Between the Reins
The Evolution of a Horseman

WRITTEN BY

Steve and Carol Huffman

Idaho

DEDICATION

This book is dedicated to Norman C. Loving,

my friend and a man I was honored to have known.

Happy Trails !
Steve & Carol
Huffman

Dear Mary & Robert,
It was so nice meeting
you! God Bless you!
Carol (& Steve)

CONTENTS

Part 1 – The Early Years

Part 2 – Unveiling

Part 3 – Turn Me Loose!

Part 4 – Deep Waters

Part 5 – The End of the Trail

* End Note*

ACKNOWLEDGMENTS

As I go to put down the finishing touches on this book, I think my wife will agree that it was a *labor of labor,* a book of my life's work during the time I was at work laboring away.

This book was started over ten years ago. That was when I was jumping off one horse after another, driving new horses to teach the all-important foundation of training, giving riding lessons or clinics, doing chores, cleaning pens, and then running in after work or on the weekends to write down a paragraph or two. And that was a good month!

The pages of this book have been "written" on the backs of horses. I owe a great deal of indebtedness to them. Some of my rides were poetic masterpieces. Some of them had all the excitement of a page-turning suspense novel. And then there were some that were downright scary. Horses are talented teachers for anyone who is united with them in the humility of learning. Being passionate about something is one thing, being *willing to learn*, quite another. The horses I rode became some of the best friends I have ever known. They were patient and fair with me as I was learning how *not* to train as well as how to train correctly. Both were essential to my education.

For someone who had never written down more than *"I love you"* on the numerous cards I gave my wife for over 40 years, I knew from the beginning that writing this book would never be possible without my beautiful partner, *the writer*. Yes, it's true. The stories are mine, but my life I shared with her. There were many nights when I would relate to her the frustration of a colt not coming around on a make-believe time frame, and she would compare it to one of her students, commenting how individual people were, that no one fit into a carbon-copy of learning all the same way. "Perhaps horses were the same," she'd muse. Sometimes, she'd tell me that maybe the horse I was training just needed a "field trip" so it could apply all it was learning. Those were the rides along ditch banks, in the desert, and outside of a classroom circle in which I learned a great deal and relaxed even more. Has writing this book been easy? No! But little by little, as I watched my wife bring my stories alive across its pages, I knew it would be worth it.

As we were writing these stories down, we couldn't resist sharing some of them with our friends. They were always encouraging, sometimes listening to chapters we had just finished, with nary a complaint. If they did feel they were under "house arrest," they never mentioned it, so we shared away!

We would like to thank our wonderful friend, Norman C. Loving, to whom this book is dedicated. For me, he was a friend in all weather, and our friendship weathered a few storms. He was the best PR man a guy could ever have, a straight shooter who always had my back. He knew all the lines in the movie, *Lonesome Dove,* and certainly exceeded the best of the character, *Gus McCrae,* when as he lay dying of cancer had more concern for me, and how I would take his loss than his own pain. He knew I was tough but that I was also tender, and he knew I would take his leaving with a broken heart. Farewell, my friend. I pray you are riding a good horse in Heaven.

To all of our friends who passed away too early, we acknowledge how much you meant to us, shaped us, encouraged us, and lived that we might know your friendship.

It was important to me that I write down my life stories for my family and also for the people who would have liked to have spent a lifetime on a horse but never got the chance. This book is for you. Enjoy!

PREFACE

Yesterday, while riding a horse in my arena, I turned around to see one of my clients, a young man in his late twenties, leaning over the fence watching me intently. He said, "You know, you have my *dream* job."

Chuckling, I responded, "It was my dream job too. Guess I'm one of the lucky ones."

Several hours (and several horses) later, his words still with me, I sat on a horse thinking how misleading training horses appears. Part of it *has* been a dream come true. There are times when I am so focused into the mind of a horse and moving them in their development that I suddenly look up and realize the sweetness of the moment, forever capturing it in my mind. I breathe in the fresh air, the open spaces, the thrill of figuring out and turning on that one proverbial *light bulb* when a horse truly understands what you are asking of them and finds freedom in their response. It is poetry, it is art in motion, and I feel fortunate to play a part in the process.

And yet, the reality of training horses has been, and always will be, just plain hard work. My business didn't happen because I dreamed it. I had to gut it out through uncertainty, frustration, danger, and toil. There were horses I rode, not by choice but to feed my family. There have been superstars, and there have been duds, and I have ridden them all. There have been horses with trauma and baggage. Climbing aboard them almost took my life. I questioned my profession and realized I had a choice: *Get in or get out.* I stayed in.

Along the way, I connected with horses, learned from and with them, and became the trainer I am today. But it has not been—in any way, shape, or form—easy. It has been, and always will be, my passion. From the time I was very young, it was generally understood by all who knew and loved me that working with horses would be my future.

That future would become the story I am here to tell today. As a professional horseman for over 50 years, I believe I finally have something to say about the dream job and living your passion. I not only have a story to tell, but life lessons to share, and an opinion based on hands-on experiences with thousands of horses. There are people, and most importantly, *horses*, which may benefit from what I have learned.

Steven K. Huffman on *Ima Sweet Chance*

Part 1
The Early Years
Chapters 1-4

1

Waiting to Begin

We are born waiting. Right up until the precise moment when we greet this world with open eyes, life then becomes a succession of small and large moments where we wait on one event to end while another begins. We wait on teeth. We wait to crawl, to walk, to talk. We wait on school, to learn to read, to graduate. We wait at traffic lights, wait on our first job, and wait to buy a house, get married, and have children. We even wait to die.

Back in the spring of 1970, the people of Huntington, West Virginia, were waiting for the rains to end but sitting on my grandmother's porch, I was waiting to begin. For years—eighteen to be exact—I had waited for this moment.

The previous summer, my best friend, Tim, had vacationed on a Colorado dude ranch. It was all he ever talked about, and I had caught his fever. Through his family's connections, we had both been hired as wranglers and horseshoers for the summer season. Unfortunately, while celebrating my high school graduation the night before, I had managed to back my parents' car into a tree, and now every piece of horseshoeing equipment I owned and needed for the most important day of my life was stuck inside the trunk. I was waiting on my dad to come help me get it open.

Tim had agreed to pick me up at my grandmother's house so I could say goodbye to her. He was due any minute to take me to my new job, and I was waiting on him. Feeling like a guy who had just robbed a bank with no way to get out of town, I wanted more than anything to get out of Huntington and begin what I knew—what I had always known—would become my life. I'd had a great childhood with a wonderful family who had given me my roots. But I knew intuitively that it could only be horses that would give me my wings. And I was ready to fly!

The only thing I knew about "the West" had been carved into my mind as a young boy by the likes of Gene Autry, Roy Rogers, and Saturday mornings watching *Sky King*. I not only dreamed about being a cowboy, I lived it the best I could while growing up in a suburban neighborhood back East. I had loved and owned horses since I had been a young boy, having many adventurous rides along the Ohio River, in apple orchards, cemeteries, and up and down every rolling road I could find. My neighborhood wasn't big enough for my passion. The entire East Coast didn't seem big enough for it either. The *West* had been calling me for as long as I could remember. It was time. I was a man, and I was ready to show the world what I knew. Or, as those older and wiser might say, what I *didn't* know.

Beavers Guest Ranch was located in Winter Park, Colorado. It was one of the largest dude ranches in the state and ran 150 head of horses. I would receive $100 a month plus $5 for every horse I shod. My friend and I would split the shoeing. Room and board was part of our payment. We were not going to get rich, but being off our parents' payroll, we needed to make our own way.

I had already realized at an early age that by loving horses, I had picked an expensive hobby. Although my parents were supportive of me, the financing for my four-legged friends had to come from my two-legged body. I cut grass with a push mower for my grandparents and anyone else up and down their street. I trimmed and edged the lawns using hand-held shears and a hatchet. I swept sidewalks, clipped bushes, ran errands, and did anything else I could do to help with the expenses of horse ownership.

Shoeing was one of those expenses. My horseshoer was an old man well into his seventies when I got to know him. He was the grandfather of one of my friends from school. I may not have listened to my teachers when I was 14, but whenever he came over, I watched and asked questions, hanging on his every word. We had a big oak tree in our back yard which provided lots of shade, and he always liked it there on those hot, humid summer nights.

One evening, he began just like he always did—trimming and rasping the hoof with skill and ease. Soon, he moved over to his portable forge and began crafting a shoe with precision and expertise. He made all his shoes by hand.

"Don't like those keg shoes," he'd say, referring to the commercially made ones that were starting to become popular. In his opinion, they may have been more convenient but not better. He had just finished nailing on the third shoe when he said the words I had been waiting on: "You wanna try and drive a few nails?"

Grinning like a kid who had just gotten his braces off, I leaped at the opportunity. From then on, every time he came to shoe he'd let me do a little more. Gradually, I began to get where I could actually shoe a whole horse. There was no way to know then that the skill he had taught me would become my ticket West.

Although I was excited, I seemed to be the only one that shared my enthusiasm. I had a close-knit family, and it was painful for my mother to watch her only son head into the great unknown. Deep inside I think she knew, maybe even before I did, that I wasn't going to come back. When she wrapped her arms around me to say goodbye, I felt her agony. She wouldn't ask me to stay, but she didn't want me to go.

My sisters, on the other hand, provided enough showers to water all of West Virginia—wailing, weeping, hugging first me, then my grandma, then each other providing enough tragedy for a *Hatfield and McCoy* stage production! Looking around at all the commotion, my dad smiled enviously, shook my hand, and let me go.

It may have been a rocky start, but once we actually left I was all eyes having never been farther west than Ohio. Every mile clicking by paraded something I had never seen before and held the promise of adventure.

We drove an old green pickup with wooden stock racks. Before horse trailers became common, it wasn't unusual to haul livestock in the back of a pickup. The wooden racks enclosed the bed and made a makeshift stall. Some horses would get so used to being hauled in a pickup truck that they could jump right into the bed from level ground! Looking back, I have to wonder how smart that was.

Although we didn't have any horses with us, we needed a place to stay each night. We tied a brown tarp to the top of the racks, and soon we had a perfect motel giving everyone we passed a true picture of West Virginia hillbillies! Our plan was to drive until we couldn't see straight and then pull over to sleep.

Food wasn't a problem because for the time being, we'd feast on Grandma's delicious home-style fried chicken she'd packed in a large paper bag. She had tucked it behind the seat like it was pure gold and, in one way, it was. Every time I got out of the truck to get gas or switch drivers, the aroma of her succulent poultry reminded me of Sunday dinners and family hugs.

Our first night, we stayed in a parking lot of a roadside convenience store somewhere in Indiana. It was a place where weary travelers could stretch their legs and get a bite to eat. By then, Grandma's "pure gold" had disappeared into our cavernous stomachs, and we were plenty hungry and exhausted from a long day's drive. Although the store was not set up for overnight parking, there wasn't a sign that said you couldn't so, to us, that meant you could. We settled in for a good night's rest.

Around 5:00 a.m., the still morning was pierced with a shrieking scream. At least, that was my interpretation of the sound. I don't know what Tim was dreaming about. Both of us were in that semi-conscious state when what you are hearing doesn't exactly match reality. It was the payphone outside of the store, ringing continuously, soon becoming apparent that it wasn't ever going to stop until *someone* answered it. We began a sort of tug-of-war, kicking each other to see who would get up.

Guess I won because Tim finally jumped out of the truck, dashed through the chilly air, picked up the receiver, and through a yawn said, "Hello?" There was a man on the other end, looking for a woman named Sadie.

"You must have the wrong number, buddy. There's no Sadie here!"

Buddy didn't appreciate Tim's answer. Irate, he demanded to know why a strange man was answering Sadie's phone early in the morning. No explanation appeased him, and he was getting pretty fired up. Finally, Tim just hung up the phone, and we got an early start and made a fast exit to our second day. The convenience store may not have cared if we slept there, but Buddy sure did, and we didn't want *him* to come looking for us!

It's funny how my mental picture of what the West *should* be kept clashing with authenticity. I couldn't wait to finally see a real sagebrush like I'd seen on *Gunsmoke,* but by the time we got through Kansas, I had seen enough.

We were somewhere close to the Colorado border when we pulled into a little café to eat. By then, we were famished and ready to eat something of substance, something our young-men bodies were craving.

"What can I git for ya?" the waitress drawled. "You boys look mighty hungry," she said, winking.

We both ordered the biggest burgers on the menu and settled into our booth waiting anxiously to inhale every last oily crumb. Soon she brought over our late-night dinner and, without hesitation, we dove in. A few minutes later, Tim motioned for her to come over.

"Can I help you with anything else?" she asked.

"Yeah, how about a hamburger?" he replied. She had forgotten the beef!

A quick apology and a long story later about a sick husband, double shifts, and a lack of sleep, she proclaimed, "There's no *way* I'm gonna have you two pay for your meal. It's *my* treat!"

We knew it would be coming out of her hard-earned tip wages, but there didn't seem to be anything we could say to change her mind. Shuffling out of the café somewhat sheepishly, we left to go find another parking lot to sleep in. But back on that waitress' table, we had placed a hefty tip to ease her anguish. Knowing we'd done a good deed made the rest of the trip smooth sailing into Denver, Colorado.

At first, the mile-high city looked like Lexington, St. Louis, Kansas City, and the rest of the big cities we had gone through—a million green and white street signs, factories blowing smog, traffic darting in and out of their lanes— hectic. We were about halfway through Denver beginning a slow rise in grade when, out of nowhere, huge snow-capped mountains jutted through the gray, hazy sky like giant carving knives slicing away at what I had known before and hurtling me straight into another world.

Winter Park, Colorado, was aptly named. We arrived in the middle of May, and I'll never forget how surprised I was to see so much snow still on the ground and on the mountains surrounding the guest ranch. It was rugged and majestic, cold, and picturesque—more beautiful than I could ever have imagined.

There were no horses at the ranch when we first arrived. They had been sent 50 miles away to winter at a lower altitude near Kremmling, Colorado. After a few days of rest, we received our first set of instructions—drive to Kremmling, find the horses in one of several large hay meadows, catch them, and shoe as many as we could each day so they would be ready for opening week the first Sunday in June.

I'm not sure what I was expecting, but the first time I laid my eyes on those horses, I was shocked. Although ugly isn't exactly the word, they were coarse at best. BIG everywhere—heads, feet, hips—just plain *big*. I had heard of the Budweiser horses, had even seen a couple of pictures of them, but I was pretty sure that these were very distant cousins to the sleek and harnessed draft horses of an eight-horse hitch. Only after many years of working with them and others like them would I come to know what I couldn't see at the moment—their big hearts.

Beavers Guest Ranch had 50 head of horses on site. The rest were leased from an organization called Sombrero

Stables which, at the time, was a very common practice for dude ranches. For a fee, you received a horse guaranteed to do the job or they would replace it with one that met your satisfaction. Each horse was branded with a number on their hip. If you liked them, you could request the same ones year after year.

The benefits to leasing horses were many. We didn't have to be out looking for horses or trying them out all the time. During the winter, when they weren't being used, we didn't have to feed them. The convenience of picking up the phone to get a replacement at any time was invaluable to our program. Once the horses were delivered to us, our part in this enterprise was to take responsibility for each horse's routine maintenance—shoeing, proper feeding, and veterinary care. Eventually, the ranch sold all of their horses to Sombrero Stables, leasing horses back from them in a partnership that lasted for over twenty years. That it was a successful one was due to the horses.

They had been purchased from everywhere with various ages and histories. Some had run the barrels, others had been roped from, and some could even rein. There were those that had been a pet, always searching for a sugar cube or a pat on the nose. All had been ridden—anywhere from feedlots, to rodeos, to someone's back yard. Whatever their experiences were with former owners, these horses had come to live in one of the most important venues of their lives.

They were given unbelievable jobs—from helping a kid from Chicago gain confidence to being the eyes of a blind person, or giving a Wall Street analyst a chance to unwind. Wherever they came from, horseflesh met humankind and left indelible hoofprints in the memories and hearts of thousands.

It was our wranglers' job to meet them. Just as the horses had come from everywhere, so did the wranglers. Some were college-bound or were already in vet school. Others were fresh off the family dairy farm, or straight out of a big city. Some had tried truck driving, waitressing, or business. All of them had unique personalities that our guests came to enjoy and looked forward to seeing again each year. The wranglers, too, seemed to be searching for that kinship they found with horses, forming attachments with certain ones that in many cases lasted for years.

Within a few weeks, every horse at Beavers Guest Ranch was given a name generally suited to their personality. There were horses for wranglers such as *Belmont, Chief,* and *Tuffy,* and horses for dudes like *Cowboy, Star,* and *Lonesome.* Women liked *Dynamite, Honey, and Angel,* and children gravitated to *Rocket, Star*, and *Cricket. Mistake* just looked funny. His ears were too big and placed atop his head backward. But he was a good dude horse, mistakes and all.

That these horses were loved is an understatement; individual guests would request the same noble steed year after year, and for one week every summer, that horse became *their* horse, free from worry, debt, or clean-up. That they were well taken care of was also an understatement. They drank from pristine rivers and grazed in lush meadows. As long as we kept plenty of feed and grain in front of them, they didn't seem to mind their current occupation.

By my third summer, it became my job, now as head wrangler, to be in charge of 150 head of horses, a crew of 15 wranglers and, most importantly, the safety of our guests. I was twenty-one years old and scared to death! Although I had always been comfortable with managing horses, it would take several years for me to become comfortable with managing people.

It was during those years that I learned to appreciate horses and their important role in this partnership of humankind and beast. You can't have one without the other. Horses don't exist as a silent partner. They're all different with individual quirks, talents, and ways of being ridden.

I remember one horse in particular. He was a deep red sorrel with four white socks and a broad white blaze on his head. He wasn't big—about 14 hands and 900 pounds. He was very quiet and easy to be around, somewhere in his late teens and showing a little age. But it didn't take much of an imagination to see that in his younger days, *Major* had been a real looker.

He arrived at the dude ranch in my fifth year and made an impact right away. It wasn't that we didn't have other good horses because we had a lot of them, but what made him so special was his versatility. He was that go-to guy, the Michael Jordan of dude horses. I could use him for my best riders knowing full well he would give them 100 percent, or I could put a novice rider on him knowing he'd give just 10 percent. Not only that, but if I had a rider with special needs, such as blindness or limited mobility, he was my safety net. He seemed to have a sixth sense about who was on him and would match his strides to their abilities rather than their disabilities. These kinds of horses don't come around very often, yet they are essential to every dude ranch or riding stable that's lucky enough to have one.

The ranch was set up on a weekly schedule. Our guests would come in on a Sunday and leave the following Sunday morning. Every Sunday afternoon, we would orientate a new group of approximately 200 riders. We offered a children's program for ages 5-12, which was a parent's dream vacation! The children were dropped off at breakfast and returned to them at dinner by our girl wranglers who doubled as the kids' program counselors. While parents were enjoying scenic rides on horseback, their children were also enjoying riding, swimming, crafts, and the best of care. There were sometimes as many as 60 kids on horseback at the same time, so assessing each child's ability and matching it to the right horse was a critical component of our program's success.

Assisting us with this enormous responsibility was *Major* whom we enlisted every Sunday to plan our weekly strategy. One by one, the children would be placed on his back, and we would watch them ride or lead them around just to determine their one perfect horse for the week. The Sunday "test drive," as we liked to think of it, became *Major's* job for the next ten years. Often, he was the first horse a child had ever ridden or even touched. It was vital to our mission and a child's well-being that he execute his drills with flawlessness.

He was a favorite among every child as being assigned *Major* for the week was an esteemed position that every one of our little privates desired. That was due to his notoriety earned in a different sort of combat zone—the Tuesday afternoon kids' rodeo. This was the day when every child became a ferocious gladiator, competing for five inches of red, white, and blue ribbons as well as green, pink, and any other color we could come up with that gave every child that glorious feeling of winning.

Our "coliseum" was an ancient wood-fenced corral, 100 feet long by 60 feet wide. The competitors, split into two teams, mounted side by side on either *Major* or a counterpart in action named *Zero* for the first of three daring and dueling races. Holding a spoon with a hard-boiled egg placed on it in one hand while gathering their reins and courage with the other hand, they sat ready on their mounts with looks of sheer determination, precariously balancing in the center of tiny saddles—30-80 pounds of featherweights waiting for the signal that would unleash their battle cry.

"Riders! Take ready! And go!"

Off they would fly down each side of the corral for 40 feet toward a barrel, dash around it, urging their champion on all the way home without dropping the egg out of the spoon. At least, that's how it was supposed to go in theory. In actuality, eggs flew everywhere, sometimes faster than the riders themselves!

The second game was to test their agility because the first game just wasn't enough. Using only the best and most expensive equipment (two sticks and two buckets placed atop two barrels), riders would once again make ready for action. The goal was to ride your horse to the barrel, exchange your stick for the one in the bucket, and ride back as fast as possible. While this race was easier on our kitchen, it sure was tough on our spectators.

"Stick! Incoming! Heads down!"

Sitting on top of the corral fence, a whole line of parents' and wranglers' heads ducked for cover like a giant wave.

After surviving the first two games, we ended our little rodeo with the classic game of apple bobbing. Once again,

the kids would ride down the corral to the other end where a
tub full of apples sat bobbing in water for each team. They
had to jump off the horse, hand it to a waiting wrangler, put
their hands behind their back, kneel down, and grab an apple
with their teeth, sprinting as fast as their little legs could go
to the finish line. Over the years, this game became my
favorite. Every child had a different method of attack on
the apples—splashing, sputtering, and half-drowning
themselves. They'd dive just like ducks searching for a
morsel in the middle of a pond, and then up they'd come
victorious. But depending on how big the smile or how tight
the grip, most of those apples fell back into the water, and
down they'd dive again.

One thing these little warriors didn't lack was
deafening noise and intense excitement as each one would
cheer on their teammates and their team's horse. And
taking them to their victory laps were *Major* and *Zero*. Since
finding another horse to match *Major's* talents was almost
impossible, *Zero* was chosen. He was trustworthy, and the
kids could guide him easily. As for speed, he was named *Zero*
for a reason measured by miles per hour, generally with a
wrangler close behind keeping him moving along.

But it was *Major*, the little red horse who was the
best. He knew the routine by heart, and even the tiniest
competitor could ride him without much assistance. Because
he was the kids' favorite, we had to alternate him in and out

of each team so that every child got to ride him or, as was repeated to me so many times, "It wouldn't be fair!" That's why I was a bit puzzled one day when it was time for the kids' afternoon ride.

Backing him out of his stall for a five-year-old boy, I was just about ready to pick up the youngster to put him into the saddle when the old horse began to stretch his joints. With a sleepy look, he let out a big wide-mouthed gaping yawn. The boy hit the ground and crawled right between my legs. As I reached around to grab him, I asked, "Where are *you* going?"

Trembling, he replied, "He ain't eatin' me!" *Major* got that afternoon off, all expenses paid, in the form of plenty of hay and no rider. Guess he knew when to play it smart. Maybe I should have named him *General*.

Although most of our guests' modern encounter with the West was in the saddle, we gave them other rewarding experiences that made their stay a richer time. Once a week, they were treated to an evening hay wagon ride. The sun would be setting behind mountains of purple majesty, casting amber waves of light across emerald green meadows as tired and horse-weary guests snuggled into cushions of sweet-smelling hay. With a slight flick of the reins, our team of horses would heave into their harness and off we'd go across the fields, swaying and bobbing along in rhythmic melody. How I enjoyed those wonder-filled evenings and the laughter of our guests as they thrilled in watching *Duke* and *Duchess* play their part in this amazing symphony. But they may have been surprised to know that those two horses who danced as one were also used as dude horses whenever the need arose.

At 16 hands, *Duchess* weighed in around 1400 pounds. *Duke* was slightly larger. Both were small for draft horses, but beautifully matched—dark chestnut, with four white socks and stars that twinkled out from the top of their heads. They had been broke to ride, but their dispositions for this task differed. *Duke* could be ridden but was much more comfortable just pulling the wagon, whereas *Duchess* would be ridden and seemed to enjoy the experience.

The barn facility had a small wooden building that I used as an office. It wasn't much, but it had been wired for electricity, and the owners had installed a telephone connected to the main office at the ranch. Their theory was that if they had a question regarding the horse program, all they had to do was call. My theory, in my infinite wisdom of now twenty-eight years of age, was that I didn't think it was fitting for real cowboys to talk on the phone, so we hardly ever answered it. Most of our guests were escaping the pressures and demands of their fast-paced, preoccupied life. Plus, I figured that *John Wayne* never talked on a phone, and he got a lot of the West won, so why should I or any of my wranglers?

If the message was important enough, they'd find a way. And they did, usually in the shape of a kid called a "chore-boy" running the quarter-mile down to the barn, huffing and puffing, to ask me their all-important question and then making the return trip a bit slower because it was all uphill on the way back. To my way of thinking, I was doing them all a favor—the kid got a chance to get out in the clean, fresh air and exercise his lungs, and the main office got a chance to put everything on pause for a bit, take a break, grab a bite to eat, savor life, if you know what I mean.

One day, the runner arrived in typical breathless fashion to ask, "Would we be able to accommodate a 350-pound man for a week of riding?" Believe it or not, in the past eight years of being head wrangler, this question had never come up. Back then, we didn't have steps or mounting blocks to help people get on their horses. If anyone had trouble, our system was to have a wrangler walk the horse over to a low spot on the ground, and as the person started up, throw their shoulders into the riders' backsides and away they'd go. Sometimes, it took two wranglers, but we always got it done.

"Three hundred and fifty pounds?" I asked. "Are you sure?" The runner assured me he was certain. "Well, how soon do you have to know?"

"Right now," he answered. "They've got him on the phone."

I shrugged. "Okay. But tell him that we have rest stops on our rides where everybody can get off their horse for a few minutes, stretch their legs, and relax. He'll probably have to stay on his horse during the breaks because we might not be able to get him back on. If he's okay with that, let's do it."

Three weeks later, on a Sunday afternoon, there he was, a little shorter than I had expected. Two undersized legs carried an oversized upper body with several generous rolls of belly hanging over his belt. But his body wasn't the only thing that was larger than life. He was one of the nicest guys you would ever want to meet and within minutes made everyone around him feel at ease. I wasn't worried in the least about accommodating him. After all, I'd been given plenty of time to prepare a plan.

He may have been big, but I had something bigger. He'd ride *Duchess*. If it could be done, she'd do it. I had 15 wranglers that worked for me—four girls and eleven guys. The plan was to get all the other riders up on their horses and out into the corral. The girls would ride out with the guests and direct traffic while the guys would meet me with *Duchess* over by a bench in the barnyard. We had purposefully placed a bale of hay in front to form a kind of make-shift step. With some assistance, the man would step up on the hay, then onto the bench, and with eleven strong young men surrounding him and the horse, he could begin his ascent up *"Mount Duchess."* He would mount from the left side, so two wranglers were assigned to the right side, and as he would climb into the saddle, they would pull the stirrup toward the ground to counter-balance his weight. The other eight wranglers would be positioned around *Duchess* to make sure she stayed in place and didn't "erupt" during the process. I would be giving instructions from behind the bench so it wouldn't tip over.

The man placed his foot into the stirrup and, with precise timing on everyone's part, the plan was executed to perfection. The only thing I hadn't planned on was the saddle. Although it was the largest one we had, it disappeared entirely under his massive body.

Oh well, I thought, *too late to do anything about that now!*

The man picked up his reins as we had instructed him and clucked. The moment of truth had arrived, and we collectively held our breath. *Duchess* took a little step then another. I was watching her ears. If they went flat against her head, that meant she was unhappy, and we were in trouble. Instead, she gingerly took two more steps, gave a little hop and barely lifted off the ground. The man didn't move an inch out of the saddle and, in fact, didn't even know that *Duchess*, who hadn't ever carried that much weight before, had instinctively tried to get rid of it. With a few more steps, she finally gained her composure and walked right into the corral.

She carried him through rivers, up and down steep mountain trails for two hours at a time twice a day for the entire week and never made a bad move. They were well-suited to each other; she would patiently stand while he would sit in the saddle without complaint during the rest stops. As he was such a kind man, the other riders would visit with him or pick wild flowers for him that he would delicately place in *Duchess's* bridle. *"Pretty is as pretty does,"* and right then, she was gorgeous.

Someone once told me that people are at their finest when they are on vacation. I was proud and inspired by the kindness our guests showed to each other. For that week, a big man with a big heart partnered with a horse of equal value and character and brought out the best in all of us.

There have always been the champions of horses: *Ivanhoe, Secretariat,* and *Seabiscuit* to name a few. As summer seasons would come and go, thousands of guests and horses would unite into a joint companionship for one week a year. I witnessed these huge, unshapely, and common dude horses transform into champions. They didn't carry soldiers into battle or win important match races, but they did carry people who came from everywhere up and down mountains in search of something one could only find on the back of a horse. The 15 summers I would spend in Winter

Park working with them would later become invaluable to me as a horseman.

My multiple experiences with various horses showed me that choosing the right horse for the right job at the right time for the right people is essential to a solid foundation on which both horse and rider can build.

Learning that has taken me thousands of horses and over fifty years. And that was something I could have never guessed I would learn when I was sitting around waiting for it all to begin.

2

Lessons

When people complain to me today about the expenses incurred by horse ownership—the price of hay, shoeing, and vet bills, not to mention buying the wrong horse for the wrong job—I have to smile. The horse business is generally learned through the pocketbook. There might be a *cash cow,* but it's *a horse of a different color* when we sadly watch our hard-earned dollars disappear into the hide and heart of that large, and always hungry, equine friend beside us.

But the greatest feature of horses—whether you own them for pleasure or you are making a living from them—is that they are talented teachers. In every experience you have with them, there will be lessons learned that, at times, can be quite costly. It wasn't any different for me in the beginning of my career with horses, and it isn't any different now. In fact, every day I work with a horse, school is still in session, and it's a class I haven't completely passed yet.

It was in 1980 that I would try my first "Fortune 500" business venture with horses. I was making a decent living and had made some extra income through some land speculations that had paid off. A happily married man with a son, and a daughter on the way, I began to reason that if Sombrero Stables could buy and lease horses and make a profit, so could I. It was a natural transition for me, and the ranch I had been working on for the past ten years was more than willing to help me get started.

They agreed to lease fifty head of horses from me for the upcoming summer, and I knew several outfitters who would lease them in the fall for hunting season. Most of their clients wanted to hunt in the back country, and the best way to get there was on horseback. As the outfitters I knew didn't own their own horses, it would be the ideal arrangement. I had just enough money to purchase what I needed if I kept to my budget.

Capitalism beats strong in American culture, and investments are generally feasible avenues by which one can improve their current financial portfolio. That is, if one knows what the heck they're doing! I thought finding the horses would be the easy part, but it was the opposite. There might have been a *Budget Car*, but a budget horse didn't exist, or was difficult to find at best.

Back then, there were no websites like DreamHorse, Craigslist, or the Internet, for that matter to help me in my search. There was only The Denver Post and miles of unfamiliar territory. It was 70 miles to Denver and 70 miles back with now four in a single-cab pickup. My wife, Carol, was chief navigator.   While preoccupying two screaming toddlers, she was reading various roadmaps and consoling me through infuriating missed exits and detours. Not to mention, my frustration with the aggressive city drivers who knew nothing about pulling a horse trailer through four lanes of gridlock. My tendency was to honk and flip them all off, which made my wife hunker down and assume protective coverage of our children. Somehow, she would manage to keep me even-tempered enough to get us out of the city alive. Then we would weave in and out of streets in every suburb only to find ourselves in the middle of nowhere staring at the first of many trials and errors.

I quickly learned what good exaggerators people were when they had a quality plug to sell. The ad had read that *Traveler* was an excellent trail horse able to carry anyone anywhere. He had been ridden in the back country and had carried packs, which to us meant he was a real find. Outfitters would love him!

Pulling into the gravel driveway of a split-level house built on the side of a hill, we scanned the small enclosed corral to find our first investment. A pony the color of chocolate lifted his head from the tire in which he was eating and greeted us with a loud, annoying whinny. He seemed to be alone. My patience, tenuous from the stressful driving, boiled over.

"What the heck is that?" I complained. "That *can't* be our horse!"

"Well, maybe there's another horse in back of that shelter," my wife soothed.

"Where?" I crabbed. "The shelter isn't any bigger than the pony!"

A middle-aged woman was making her way to our truck from the house. Overweight, she was limping and explained during her sales pitch that she would still be riding *Traveler* but for her knee surgery and bad back. He was quiet, willing, and a sweet little horse.

"Horse?" I scoffed, and my wife shushed me.

The woman cocked her head, eyeing me with suspicion, then looked at my kids and my wife smiling sweetly and said, "Well, I guess you can have them both for $300."

"*Both*?" my wife questioned.

"Well, yeah, they can't be separated," the woman explained, adding wistfully, "They've been together since *Traveler* was a baby. Our other horse is right over there."

I looked in the direction she was pointing. My wife squinted, and our kids peeped out over the dashboard. There was a flash of gray tail swishing around the backside of the house, the fine print of the ad you never read. And there, standing sort of propped up against one wall resting in the shade was a white behemoth sack-of-bones gelding. Eyes, rimmed in pink, popped out from a head that would rival his ancient ancestors. We were about 20 years too late to get any action out of him, and I was about 20 seconds from coming unwound and telling this woman what I *really* thought of her two-for-one package deal.

 Pulling me close, my wife whispered, "Couldn't we use the pony as a kid's horse? And who knows, maybe the big guy's a diamond in the rough."

"Yeah, a chunk of coal, maybe," I retorted.

She was right, of course. Horses for kids were hard to come by. Maybe it was because I was tired, hungry, and didn't want to leave empty-handed, but I decided to take a chance on them, figuring the old guy didn't have too much longer to hold up shelters.

We renamed *Traveler* to *Wimpy* right on the spot and named the gelding *Popeye*, fed him a lot of "spinach," and found out he was what everyone needed their first time on horseback—a push-button machine that *would* take anyone anywhere. *Wimpy* may or may not have packed game in the back country, but he sure packed a ton of kids. And every evening, as hundreds of horses were turned out from their long days of carrying dudes, first the kids' horses then the others, he would stand at the gate that led into the cool, green pasture waiting on his best friend, *Popeye*. Sometimes, you've got to polish the diamonds to see them glitter.

Those were our good investments. But there were plenty of trips to Denver, Fort Collins, Colorado Springs, and every small town in between that didn't pay off at all. There had to be an easier way to buy 48 more horses. So I did what all adventure capitalists do—I asked advice from those in the know. The men who ran *Sombrero Stables* were full of it.

"Sale barn," one said to me. Another round of learning was about to begin.

I had no real experience in buying horses through a sale barn although I had been to a few as a kid. Even though I had never been an active participant in the buying process, I wasn't too worried. That's the great thing about youth—it requires no experience. I was a young man with money in my pocket, and that right there should have been a red flag for danger, but no one tried to stop me.

To be honest, going to those late-night horse sales was the highlight of my life. I don't know what it is about a sale barn, especially the old ones where you sit in an oval-shaped coliseum in uncomfortable folding metal chairs with the smell of smoke and horse encircling your whole body in a sort of halo.

Everyone looks the same. No matter where you go, you'll see the same familiar scene—the fat bald man smoking, the tall skinny guy in front of you that you can't see around, the guy with the bigger-than-Texas cowboy hat, and the ancient of ancient Marlboro men that look and smell of leather.

There is an air, a presence even, that to a horseman can become quite addicting. You know there is a hidden treasure amidst all of the horses taking their turn at running through that small circular ring, and you know that this night, you will find your one special horse.

At first, I bought several of those special horses. There was the horse with the big knee, the horse that became navicular the next day, the horse that was blind in one eye, and that very special horse with no teeth. I was right on target to be broke in no time, but I couldn't stop.

It was always so mind boggling to me that before the sale began, you had an opportunity to look at all of the horses outside. They all looked common and plain and yet, once they appeared inside that tiny ring with the lights illuminating them through the bluish-gray smoke from above, there was instant transformation. The nag out back became a prospect, and you had seconds to decide if this was the one. The bidding begins and you're wondering what the guy sitting next to, above, or below you knows that you don't. Suddenly, your hand shoots up, and they call your number, and you just bought her, whatever she is. It might be several days before you know exactly what you have, but as you go outside to load her up that night, all you can hope for is that she'll look better in the morning. Kind of like marrying a blind date—like it or not, she's yours.

A few horse sales and thousands of dollars later, I began to change my ways. I had had enough of blind dates. I began to pay more attention to details. I glued my eyes on every leg, joint, or crooked foot. I scanned every inch of horse flesh and trained myself to see every bump and scar. And I dang made sure they all had teeth! Writing the numbers down from the ones I liked outside, I only bid on those horses that met my utmost approval, regardless of the kid who unbridled, unsaddled, and slid off their rumps, walking under their belly. Trick-riding didn't impress me. A well-balanced horse did.

Slowly, I was catching on to the tricks of the trade. A seasoned rider, by using the side of the ring, could make a horse look broke better than it was. A roached mane could make a horse's neck appear thinner and a caveson could make the head look shorter. A longer saddle blanket could make the back look short-coupled, and a braided tail could make the hindquarters look bigger. And I never underestimated the power of a pretty girl on a horse. They were all little things that could become big mistakes when quick decisions were required.

Every time I would purchase a new horse, I would learn something. Take the horse that was blind in one eye, for example. Once I got him home and discovered what I had done, I realized, due to liability issues, it would not be wise to use him for a dude horse. But a wrangler's horse was a possibility as they were more skilled and seasoned riders. A deep auburn with a white blaze streaking down his face, he *was* striking. Carrying himself with great confidence, he required a noble and suitable name, but both my wife and I drew a blank.

We started throwing out all sorts of names that had to do with anything that he looked like or some sort of character we could attach to him. We couldn't name him *King, Prince, or Captain.* They were far too common. *Pirate, Red Beard,* or *Patch* brought visions of horses far too mischievous.

"How about *Jack*?" I suggested.

"You want to name a horse after your father?" she asked.

"No," I laughed, "You know . . . as in **one-eyed** Jack?"

"When you're playing cards, aren't one-eyed Jacks wild?" she asked. And so, that name came and went along with the others.

But the name *Jack* triggered some distant memory in my wife, and she sat up suddenly asking, "Hey! What's the name of that actor that always plays in the cowboy movies—you know, sometimes he's a good guy, sometimes bad. He's got kind of a strange eye . . . Eli?" she paused, thinking.

"You mean Jack Elam?" I asked.

"Yeah, yeah! That's him!" she said.

"You want to call this horse *Eli*?" I asked.

"No, I want to call him *Whitney* . . . as in Eli Whitney," she answered matter-of-factly, as if the connection between the inventor of the cotton gin and Jack Elam was a very natural correlation. "He really was a creative genius and visionary. Plus, he helped make life a lot easier for a lot of people. Maybe this horse will help people too. It won't hurt to give him a name of someone so far-sighted when he's short one eye." she mused.

I don't know why *Whitney* stuck, but it did. And for some strange reason, it fit. Besides, there was already a horse at the ranch named *Eli*, but I don't think my wife knew that, and I didn't have the heart to tell her.

For one whole summer, the wranglers used *Whitney* as their lead horse, and it didn't take long for him to win them over, becoming one of their favorites, one eye and all. He compensated for his loss of vision by turning his head slightly to the right and seldom shied at unexpected sights and sounds. He had been well-trained at some point in his life and was a natural athlete and could outpace every other wrangler horse.

That fall, I was shoeing some horses, getting them ready for hunting season, when a friend of mine stopped by to talk. Bill was one of Winter Park's local businessmen who had recently retired and was looking for something to do or someone to visit. I had met him in our local hardware store where he frequented, and our personalities had clicked. He liked a good joke, and so did I. After a while, he began to tell me that he was looking for a horse. He had ridden a lot as a kid and although he hadn't in a while, he thought he might like to take it up again. I knew I couldn't keep *Whitney* forever because sooner or later someone might get hurt, and that wasn't a chance I wanted to take. But still, he was such a solid horse in so many ways; I hated to see him go to waste.

"I've got just the horse—perfect in every way—except he has only one eye," I said.

Bill hit his knees, laughing. "Think I'll keep looking if you don't mind!"

Several weeks later, I had some horses to deliver to a hunting camp. Mine had to be sorted out from 100 head of horses, all running together in a big open meadow two miles from the ranch. Nestled between the towns of Winter Park and Fraser, *Maryvale Meadow* was a slice of Heaven with lush green grass and a natural stream running through it. Area locals referred to it as the last bit of paradise not being bought up and sectioned off for condominiums. Some of the other guest ranches rotated stock that needed extra rest or recuperation in and out of *Maryvale* to keep them fresh and well-fed. In order to sort mine from the bunch, the entire herd of horses had to be rounded up and drove into a makeshift holding pen. Then, I had to catch each one of my horses, tie them to one of the trees surrounding the pen, and load them into my stock trailer.

Usually, getting someone to help me was not a problem as any of my friends loved playing cowboy, but it seemed that on that particular day, no one was available. I found Bill in the local coffee shop. He was thrilled I'd asked him, and we agreed to meet each other at *Maryvale* the next morning.

When he arrived, I had two horses saddled up, ready to use to round up the others. Those horses weren't too keen to leave their breakfast and coupled with Bill's inexperience, it took us a several hours to have them gathered in the pen ready to sort.

Looking through my bunch of horses, Bill asked, "Where's that blind one-eyed horse?"

"Right there," I answered, pointing to his horse. "You're on him!"

The next day, there was a knock on my door. It was Bill.

"What would you take for that horse?" he asked.

"What would you give?" I answered.

"Well, not as much as I would if he had *two* eyes!" he said laughing. We made a deal, and Bill came that afternoon to pick *Whitney* up.

I happened to be in the hardware store the next summer getting supplies for opening day when Bill came in. I hadn't seen or heard from him in a while and was a bit apprehensive, thinking maybe the horse hadn't worked out for him.

But after a warm return of my greeting, I plunged in. "How's that one-eyed horse doing, Bill? Have you had any problems with him?" I asked.

"Not one bit!" he answered and winked. "As long as I keep his head turned with his good eye facing front, we go anywhere. I've even run him through groves of aspen, and he's pretty wiry. He darts in and out and around them like he doesn't even *see* them!" he laughed.

Bill rode and enjoyed *Whitney* for five more years. Every time I would see him, he would thank me for selling him his one-eyed friend. Eventually, health issues forced Bill to sell the horse. A few years later, Bill died of pancreatic cancer. But he would always remember the times he spent on *Eli Whitney*—the horse named after the famous inventor—as a dream come true.

There are times when the right horse for the right job and the right person comes as an unexpected gift—priceless in value. *Whitney* was far from perfect. But like they say, "Beauty is in the *eye* of the beholder."

3

Out of the Box

Eventually, all my late-night sale barns paid off. I began putting together a pretty decent string of dude horses, not to mention the beautiful, young colts I couldn't resist buying. I knew nothing about starting them and really didn't care because even though I might have been lacking in skills, when it came to guts, I was a natural *Kamikaze* pilot. As soon as I could find a dry spot somewhere, I would start riding, putting as much time on them as I could before the dude season would begin. We weren't at peak capacity until the first of July, which gave me a month or so more to put one of my wranglers on them.

At first, all I was after was that a potential dude horse would learn to relax. I would have the wrangler just follow one of our outgoing rides with them in which they would cross plenty of rivers and walk up and down mountain trails. We could get them four or five hours of riding a day where they saw and heard plenty of strange and unidentifiable objects—boulders to look at and go around, birds fluttering, chipmunks chattering, wind blowing through trees, and branches snapping, not to mention whistles, laughter, and the voices of others in front of them.

Not only that, but they were learning to eat on breaks and how to stand in stalls while waiting on a ride. In a couple of weeks, we could lead rides with them instead of just having them follow, and by the middle of July, they were packing dudes. I don't remember one time this didn't work, and I was getting better at buying the horses with the right temperaments for the job.

By the end of hunting season, these horses were pretty solid with their surroundings. Sometimes, I would sell these young horses to a local buyer who liked them. He could never understand how I was getting these young colts so seasoned. This was a nice option for me because I didn't have to winter so many horses and, after all, I was trying to run a business. It wasn't all about money, but if I could make a profit, it made good sense to me. Not to mention, it would give me another excuse to go to the sale barn the next spring to buy more pretty colts.

After a few years of starting these young horses, anytime someone would make a big deal about how hard it was to start a colt, it would puzzle me as to why they thought it difficult. It was easy for me. I didn't understand then what I do now. I was making a one-dimensional horse, suitable for the one specific purpose of being a safe trail horse. At that time, I had never even heard of the cliché, *getting out of the box*, but after years of being in a box I didn't even know I was in, I was about to get out.

The local rodeo club offered Wednesday night roping. I had never roped before but had several friends who did, and they all encouraged me to try. I was addicted immediately, and that whole summer, I was like *any* new roper—hard on the ones they love, especially dogs and children. I'd pick up my rope to practice, and they'd run for cover! I'm not sure what throwing a rope at something over and over again does to a brain. Although I'm not a psychiatrist, I'm sure it can't be anything good. Once you get the fever, you become like any other type of junkie—your heart starts pumping, your hands start to sweat, everyone and everything around you is a blur, but what separates you from the rest is it's hard to hide your addiction. After all, you have a rope in your hand, and you're mounted on a horse. It was during one of those Wednesday night *prayer ropings,* as I called them (because it was only through the grace of God that I would ever catch anything), that events in my comfortable boxed-in world began to change.

I had been riding a borrowed, old white gelding who had been used by many a seasoned roper on thousands of cattle. The only problem was *Old Whitie* wasn't as fast as he once was and the cattle we were using seemed to be having a lot of fun outrunning him. I really didn't think too much about it as it was what it was, and I was just enjoying myself being there. However, after a while, everyone started feeling sorry for me, and as I would ride into the roping box, they would all begin to coach me to ride a little harder, throw a little faster. Occasionally, someone would get behind *Whitie* and tap him on the rump trying to get him to run out of the box a little quicker. Although their intentions were good, usually something would go wrong—*Whitie* might run a little faster, but then I'd get excited and make a bad throw, or I'd get myself geared up to make a good throw, and *Whitie* would decide not to run. Or, I would rope myself or the gate, or *Whitie's* tail, or anything that would come too close to my wayward loop . . . anything but a cow that is!

There was a man who worked the chutes for us who had just moved into our community. One day, he showed up with a truck and trailer, and as I was walking by to get my horse, he was unloading. He handed me the reins to one of his horses and said, "Try this one today. I think you'll like him." I was a little taken aback by his gesture, but thought, *Why not? I sure know Whitie would appreciate a break.*

He was a plain brown horse, very common looking, but as I began to lope him around the arena, getting the feel for him, I liked him right away. He was well-broke, lots of handle, and very responsive. As I backed him into the box, it became clear he was all business. Back bowed, muscles began to tighten, rippling down the length of his body, his eyes glued on the cow making its way down the chute. His ears flickered ever so slightly back and forth, listening for the gate to open. Instinctively, I grabbed the horn. He was telling me *this ride would be different.* I wasn't in Kansas anymore.

Adrenalin at full capacity, I had to question, *Had I made a mistake?* Maybe *Old Whitie* wasn't that bad after all. I called for my steer, and we are off and running. The horse was faster than any horse I had ever been on. In an instant, there I was—side by side a beautiful pair of horns. No more reaching, stretching, grunting; they were right there. I threw, and my loop rang true. As the rope began to tighten, I wrapped it around my saddle horn, and my horse veered to the left. When the steer's weight reached the end of the rope, the horse dug in—legs churning, tunneling the arena ground in a sort of tug of war where I knew the steer would never win against such a powerful opponent.

I was right; the cow began to slow down and my heeler came in roping his back legs. A cheer arose from my little crowd of supporters. Now, I was really hooked.

However, I knew it wasn't my skill that caught that night. Nothing there had changed but the horse. He had made it so much easier for me. I could concentrate more on roping and less on getting there or not. His name was *Bartender* and just like the real ones he listened, and I was thirsty for more.

When roping was over that night, I gave the man back his horse. As we began to talk, I found out he was taking care of a ranch down the road and breaking some colts on the side. A few days later, I decided I'd go see what was going on at his ranch. The entrance gate was closed. On it hung a *No Trespassing* sign. Parking my truck, I went and sat on top of the gate. I felt a little uneasy, but then I began looking around. I could see someone riding a horse in a round pen. Sliding off the gate, I walked toward it.

As I came into his sight, the man who had been so friendly at the roping said to me in a hardened voice, "Can't you read?"

It was obvious I was not welcome. The air got pretty thick for a moment, and I started to leave, but for some reason I didn't want to. Making small talk, I asked him about the colt he was riding and if he liked the area. Things started to relax, and he began to work the colt again in the pen.

I was amazed at what I saw. There was motion, but it was fluid, smooth, graceful—even elegant. I could not separate the two as horse and rider became one. There was something going on here, and even if I wasn't welcome, I wasn't going to leave. I stayed and watched him work a couple more colts. When I finally did leave to go home, I could not forget what I had just seen.

This was different than the way I was starting colts and so were the results. It was more than just transportation; it was something I never even knew existed. Beyond skill and talent, it was art—at its finest. It moved me, stirring what I thought I knew about horses onto a blank canvas, and I wasn't even sure how to pick up the brush.

I had played sports all through my school years and had been coached in the fundamentals of body control and timing and how important it was to learn correct techniques. My mind kept coming back to the comparison. The man's young horses had the look of athletes in training. They were waiting, listening, and learning, and so was I.

Back at his ranch the next day, I never even hesitated. Springing over the gate, I strolled toward the round pen. The rider looked at me, shook his head, and said, "I know, you just can't help yourself, can ya?"

"Nope," I grinned, and for some reason, he let me stay. I watched as he rode several colts, and then he saddled a black one that was very thoroughbred-looking.

He said, "This one belongs to a friend of yours. I'm sure he wouldn't mind if you gave him a try."

All I did *was* try. What looked so easy, so smooth, and effortless when the man was riding, quickly turned into confusion and frustration for both me and the colt. Standing on the ground watching, it had been impossible to detect the subtleness of it all—the exact timing, the balance, two working as one. This was like getting out of a Volkswagon bug into a Ferrari—a well-tuned machine. I'd push the brakes, then the accelerator, then I'd overcorrect. It was a bumpy ride. I was over my head and certainly over my skill level, but I loved it. I have to admit I was more than a little embarrassed that day. I had thought I was a better rider, but after that performance, it became apparent to me that it's never what you know that gets you into trouble, it's what you think you know.

I had a friend once who owned what we thought was a pretty good horse. He had him up for sale and sold him to a guy that was looking for a ranch horse. When I questioned if he had gotten his price he answered, "Nah."

I asked him, "Well, did you show him all the horse could do?"

With a slow reply he answered, "Yeah, that was the problem. I showed him everything the horse could do, and the guy showed me everything he *couldn't* do. I figured just the information was worth something."

That's how we learn. Although in something such as training a horse, I believe it can't be fully taught or learned. It must be felt. It can't happen until you've been shown that there is a bigger picture, a clearer vision off canvas and out of your box. For me, I knew then that while riding horses had been my passion, learning how to train them would become my mission. Finger painting is one way to create a picture, but for me, it was how I would learn to hold the brush that would create my masterpiece.

4

A New Chapter

There are a lot of sayings about the stages of life such as, "All good things must come to an end," and "Nothing stays the same forever," and this would begin to come true for me as well. My time in Winter Park was coming to an end, and a new chapter in life would begin. Beavers Guest Ranch was now on its third owners, and it was becoming clear that the current new owners were more interested in land development rather than running a dude ranch. After a couple of years, they decided it was in their best interest to close it down.

I hung around the area for a few more years. One summer, I ran a small dude string for a condominium association. It was a little like the old westerns meeting the new trendsetters. Right in the middle of the condominium complex was a plush outdoor pool/jacuzzi facility complete with state-of- the-art exercise equipment and a 5-star restaurant. And just past the tidy, white-picketed fence was our rough and tumble rickety horse corral with 15 head of tail-swishing, feet-stomping, whinny-bellowing, manure-making horses tied to it. But hey! There's always a little piece of Heaven somewhere, right? And for that summer, the trendsetters rode a lot of miles on our safe and reliable "angels in disguise."

As I had branched out into my own dude string of horses, and winter was long in Winter Park, it was natural for me to try running my own sleigh ride. Once again, my entrepreneurial spirit caught hold of me, and I offered a couple sleigh rides in two different locations. One served hot chocolate by an outdoor fire, and the other served a five-course dinner in a barn with live entertainment. I truly enjoyed driving those big horses. We had always had a team or two at the ranch for our evening hay-wagon rides, so I had experience driving teams.

But it sure is different driving a team on dirt than on snow. At first, I was like a Texan in a snowstorm. I got stuck a lot! But after several rides, the sleigh runners blazed a wide berth across the trail of hard-packed snow. The challenge then was to stay on that pack. Early in the season, that wasn't such a problem, but as snowstorms came and went, piling several more feet of snow on top, it became a trial and my utmost responsibility to keep the runners in the hard-packed tracks of snow. If the horses ever came off, they'd plunge belly deep into fresh fallen snow, wallowing, floundering, and lurching through it, which gave new meaning to the wintertime experience of "dashing through the snow." Not to mention, it always seemed to be snowing at night, and at $^-40°$ to $^-50°$, it was cold. Sometimes during a snowstorm, all I could do was give the horses their heads and hope for the best. More times than not, the less I helped, the better it was.

Christmas was always a busy time of year in the sleigh-ride business. I kept three teams. During those peak times, I would alternate them in to keep the horses as fresh as possible. I offered two rides a night, and they were full for the whole month. It was a time that could make or break profit margins.

Naturally, according to Newton, if anything could go wrong, it would. When one of my big draft horses got hurt and was unable to work, I pushed the panic button. I had always prided myself in having a back-up plan, but I had already checked off plans A, B, and C and was ziplining toward Z when a name popped into my head. I didn't know what to do, but I knew who did. A wise man doesn't always have the answers; he just knows where to get them.

Seconds later, I was on the phone to Rex Walker, owner of Sombrero Stables. Over the years of leasing horses from him for the ranch, he had proven that whenever I needed something, he could deliver. If anyone could help me, he could.

"Rex?" I said, "I'm in trouble. I got a horse down, and I need a team by 5:00 tonight!"

With a slow and laid backed voice, he answered, "Don't everybody?"

It must have been the desperation in my voice that he heard because he agreed to try and find another team, with no promises. As I hung up the phone, all I could do was wait and hope. Of all the days, that was the day I had chosen to drive to Denver for some supplies so Bruce, the young man that worked for me, would be at the ranch to receive the horses from Rex.

I was a nervous wreck all day, constantly worrying and wondering if a team would be there when I got back. That was back before phones were readily imbedded into everyone's hip, so texting wasn't even an option I could have ever imagined except perhaps on an episode of *My Favorite Martian.*

When I finally drove into the ranch around 4:00, I saw Bruce frantically adjusting harnesses, and that was not a good sign. More panic set in.

"Is the team here?" I asked, not quite sure I wanted to hear the answer.

"Well, yeah," Bruce answered, pausing slightly. He continued, "Kind of."

Just as I was pondering what exactly "kind of" meant, with a tiny tick of his head toward the barn, he added, "Come and see for yourself."

Bruce was a big kid—6'4" and about 240 pounds. I followed him into the dark barn, and as my eyes began to adjust, there appeared two beautiful mares—chestnut colored with flax manes and tails—perfect in every way except that standing next to Bruce, they looked like midgets. In fact, standing next to *me*, they *were* midgets!

"Holy cow!" I yelled, "These are ponies!" To the phone I ran. I didn't have speed dial but I'm pretty certain my fingers never found digits so fast.

"Rex! Are you out of your mind? There's 24 people in our sled! They're paid in full and due in here in about 30 minutes!"

Once again, in his characteristic slow drawl, he answered, "I think they can do it. Besides, they're all I've got."

I hung up, nodded to Bruce and said, "Put on the Santa suit. We're gonna' give 'em a try. *Ho! Ho! Ho!*"

Bruce shrugged and went to go get his costume. He got paid whether the team could pull or not. It was me left standing in the icy cold dark wondering how I could afford to refund 24 people their money and how many little kids I was going to disappoint. Where was Rudolph when you needed him? I sure could have used his magic right about then or, at the very least, some of the stuff that *really* made Santa's nose so red. What I truly needed was nothing short of a Christmas miracle.

And then it happened. No, I didn't hear the heavenly angels' choir or see visions of sugar-plum fairies, but as I stood there, I thought of a line Jimmy Stewart delivered in a movie once. "If you don't try, then you don't do," and I realized trying was all I could do at that moment. I'd worried enough; it was time to do. Driving those big teams had always been my favorite part of the sleigh ride business, and this evening, though uncertain, was no exception.

No one was around; the only sounds penetrating the deep silence were the clinking of the chains and the rustle of the leather harness I threw onto the backs of the two little mares. Hitching them up, I walked one horse over the tongue and the other into its place beside her. There they stood like obedient servants as I hooked the chains to the doubletree. Santa appeared beside me, took the reins, and with one final look of despair climbed into the sled.

We could hear the guests coming down the lane laughing all the way, if you know what I mean. No time for a trial run. It was do or die trying. As I loaded the guests into the sled, I could feel the sweat rolling off my neck. Would they . . . could they pull? Sure was a lot of weight. I backed away from the sled and forced myself to watch.

The little mares had seemed quiet and gentle, but as soon as Bruce clucked to them, I couldn't believe what I saw. Like a scene straight out of Hollywood, those two little mares dropped to their knees and, with precise split-second timing, leaped into their harness with the force that could tear a tree from its roots. The sled lurched, and bang! They were off— hooves throwing snow everywhere! It's hard to explain what it was like to see such massive power; the energy and beauty of these two horses working in unison could only be summed up in one word *magnificent.*

Stars stretched across the night sky, and the moon cast just enough vision across glistening white meadows. The sounds and pictures of the creaking of the wooden sled, sleigh bells ringing, watching a 6'4" Santa Claus hand out candy canes, and the melody of laughter from 24 guests will stay in my heart and mind forever.

We kept the ponies the rest of the season. They soon became Bruce's favorite team, never once failing to get the job done. In early March, with about one month to go in the sleigh-ride business, the little mares surprised us once again. One spring day as we were harnessing them for their nightly work, I noticed that one of the mares' udders appeared to be swollen. I ran over to look at the other mare. Her udders were swollen too! It could only mean one thing.

"These ponies are *pregnant!*" I yelled to Bruce. I was right. Come April, they each had a filly colt. I've often thought about them and how those two little mares gave a whole new meaning to the phrase "working mothers." In fact, I think they taught me a lot about work ethic—work as a team, put your head down, and brave the future. What I didn't know then was that futures can change.

My years in Winter Park were a lot of fun, but the economic climate of the late 1980s was changing, and I knew intuitively that it would only get worse. The life I had known for years was changing too, and my wife and I felt we needed a new direction, not only for us but for our two children as well. I guess we took "new direction" literally because we sold almost everything we had, packing the rest into the back of a used, rusty 30-foot goose-necked horse trailer, and moved back East to work with my dad.

My father was then superintendent of one of the largest and most historical cemeteries outside of Pittsburgh. I don't know what I was thinking. In a few short months, I was miserable—not enough horses and way too many people. I remembered then why I had left!

As another Christmas time came into focus, I realized that only one year before, I had stood in a mountain meadow wielding the reins of a mighty team trudging through drifts of snow. Collective memories of the hundreds of horses I had touched, ridden, and learned from in Colorado reeled through my mind. I could feel a familiar restlessness urging me, propelling me to go back West.

Cemetery management had been my father's career path, and he was unbelievably good at it, but it wasn't mine. I had tried to change myself into something I wasn't, and it *wasn't* working. I had no idea how to get back West or if working with horses would be economically sound for me and my family, but I knew it was a future on which we could build.

My wife sent out our annual Christmas letter describing our current situation. Actually, I think she called it a wrong turn. A few months later, a friend I had worked with in Colorado called me. He had remembered my wife's Christmas letter. He said he now lived in Idaho, and he and his wife had some Morgan horses and were looking into starting a horse-boarding facility, and asked if I would be interested in taking care of the place and doing some training. Those were the words I had been waiting on. And just like the line from the old editorial, I thought, "Yes, Virginia, there IS a Santa Claus!"

Part 2
Unveiling
Chapters 5-9

5

Unveiling

We arrived in Kuna, Idaho, in the fall of 1987 and in a short period of time, my debut as a professional horse trainer began. Through contacts of my friends, I began to get in a horse or two to train. We were also getting in a few horses to board. Winter would soon arrive, and the serious horse people were looking for an indoor arena that had lights so they could ride in the evening after work and on the weekends. Our facility was very nice, and we filled up quickly. This was a good balance for me; I could take care of the boarding horses in the morning with feeding, cleaning, turn-outs, and other chores, and in the afternoons, I would ride my training horses getting done before the boarders came to use the arena at night.

Although I wasn't a real horse trainer, so to speak, by now I had been around a lot of horses. Between the ones I had as a kid, those at the guest ranch, and my own horses that I had purchased for my leasing business, I was confident I could handle anything that might come my way. After all, I had a bit of experience starting colts, and what little I had learned from the man in Colorado, I thought, *"How hard could it be?"*

I would soon learn that it is one thing to train your own horses on your own time schedule with your own expectations, and quite another thing to train for money. Money changes everything. Now I was working on someone else's payroll, someone else's schedule and, not to mention, someone else's expectations. Those seemed to vary with each client. I really didn't know what was expected of me or what I could expect of a horse. I knew nothing about time frames— what a horse could learn in 30 or 60 days or what was even feasible for one to learn. I soon found myself in a real mess. I was riding horses I didn't get to pick, on a time frame I couldn't control, all for a passion and paycheck.

As a new trainer, I rode everything that came my way, and they weren't all great. Their personalities were all over the map and so were their abilities. But every horse I rode, I would try to make as light as I could. I really didn't know how to do that, but in Colorado I had learned the next best thing—it was possible. It was hard to make some of these horses light because they were all kinds of breeds and temperaments—from race horses to mustangs—but also from different environments.

The importance of the environment in which a horse is raised and handled is no different from that of a child. Any teacher will tell you that sometimes little Johnny is not always the bundle of joy his parents think he is once he gets away from home and is asked to do something he doesn't feel like doing. But whether the owner would bring me a spoiled Betty or runaway Bart, they always left me with these sincere words of assurance, "I'm sure *my* horse will be easy." Horse training is a well-rounded education. You will always have your "*Make-Me*" or your "*Show-Me*" horse and everything in between, but I don't think I ever had an easy one, only some easier than others.

It takes three things to make a good horse, the first one being a good horse. The second is time, and the third is skill. Without all three of these things, you are doomed to a world of frustration. What can I say? Welcome to *my* world! During the 1980s and 1990s, there was a methodology going around that horse training was putting a horse in a trap and teaching it how to get out. Although I think there is some merit to that way of thinking, it has been my experience that if you're going to put a horse in a trap, you sure better know how to get him out! For instance, if you want to teach a horse to back-up, you might try riding him up into a fence until he gets the idea he can't go through the fence and decides to back up. It sounds simple and can work on many horses. But then, there are always those who decide to go over the fence, or even under it, the ones that decide to side-pass around it, or the worst ones—the ones that decide to rear up and then decide they like it. Who's trapped now? In the early years, I'm not sure I was learning how to train a horse or how not to. *Both* were essential to my education.

One time, I was trying to get a horse to stop without much success. A friend of mine was watching me, and I asked him why he thought it wasn't stopping.

He replied, "I don't know why he isn't stopping, but I do know that what you are doing isn't working."

Truer words were never spoken. I couldn't help but think back to a time when as a young boy, I was trying to shut a cabinet drawer in the kitchen, and it would not close. Over and over, I would shove harder and harder without any success.

I was caught up in the moment until finally, hearing the commotion, my dad came into the kitchen and said, "Son, when a drawer won't shut, there's usually a reason." He got down on one knee to investigate the problem, and in a few seconds had the answer. A small match was wedged in the mechanism of the drawer making it impossible to shut.

I figured the same could be true for horses. Maybe there was a reason they wouldn't stop, turn, or listen. If I would just stop, turn, or listen, then I would discover the problem. Once again, I would soon learn that I could stop, turn, and listen all I wanted, but training a horse and fixing a cabinet drawer were two different things, the main problem being that a cabinet drawer doesn't have a brain and two eyes staring back at you thinking, "If I stop, turn, and listen, I can outthink or outscare this guy, and he will go away and leave me alone." And believe me, there were many times when I wanted to do just that!

Although there are occasions where you must take time to problem solve and evaluate the reason for the horse's behavior, it is also imperative that you realize that training is a process that cannot be cheated. That is, if one wishes to achieve the highest standards according to the horse's ability. As I rode horse after horse, I was beginning to realize this. Even though I hadn't grasped the enormity of this concept, I was starting to put together what I would later refer to as the *ABC's* to training. They would become part of my foundational approach to training as I was growing in understanding that the alphabet doesn't begin with Z!

"Back to basics" is a phrase I borrowed from my school teacher wife. But before you can get back to *it*, you've got to learn what *it* is and where *it* needs to go. You don't learn the tricks of the trade in horse training. You learn the trade.

6

Baptism

I was enjoying everything about training a horse except getting bucked off. Even though I'd had plenty of opportunities to ride bucking horses back in Colorado, at the ranch and in local rodeos, the saying, "Ain't a horse that can't be rode, ain't a cowboy who can't be thrown," is something every professional horse trainer deals with every day.

There were those days when I was quite the bronc rider. Then there were those days when it wouldn't take much, and I was in the dirt. Everyone who rides a horse has to accept the fact that at any time, the possibility of getting bucked off is real. I don't believe there is such a thing as a completely "bullet-proof" horse. They can all get spooked, have a cranky day, or say no once in a while. I have a good friend who has been coming over to ride at my place for the last 20 years. He says he can tell me every hard spot on my property.

If you go to a professional football game and a player gets hurt, there is help immediately. Even a professional bull rider has access to assistance, not to mention when they do get up, there are cheers and sympathy from the crowd and, at least in the football player's case, a nice, refreshing squirt of *Gatorade*.

Once, I had been riding a big paint stud horse for about ninety days, and he was coming along just fine. I warmed him up every day in the round pen, but since he seemed to be getting a little on the lazy side, I decided to just hop on one day. A fellow never knows when school is going to be in session. I was about to learn the lesson of a lifetime.

I can't remember whether we went two steps or three before he put his head between his legs, let out a squeal, and bucked like a wild man. I hit the ground and bounced at least four times. I couldn't get up; I couldn't even breathe, and a light in my head kept flashing on and off. As I lay there, I kept hoping someone would show up just to check me out, help me up or, at the very least, give me a squirt of *Gatorade*.

Another time, after I got bucked off, a cowboy friend of mine had shown up in time to see the action. He stood over me looking down, and as I lay there gasping for air, he said, "I know just how you feel," then caught my horse, tied it to the fence, and added, "See you later!" So much for the sympathetic, cheering crowd!

When you train horses for a living like I do—a one-man operation—you are alone most of the time, so no one sees a lot of the embarrassing things or the neat things. One day, while my wife was working in our yard, a horse threw me so high, I felt like I was ejected from a cockpit. I came down feet first, landed on his rump, and jumped gracefully to the ground.

I yelled to my wife, "Wow! Did you *see* that?"

Looking around, she stood up from her flowerbed and asked, "See what?"

Oh, well. Even the cheerleader was looking the other way that day.

There is a high desert climate where I live in Idaho. It is also an area where farming yields cash crops, and to assist in transporting the water to the fields, we have a lot of irrigation canals. Next to each canal will be dirt or gravel service roads that are lightly traveled by vehicles. They can be nice places to ride a horse and put some miles on them outside of an arena. One of the largest is known as the New York Canal. Its service road goes for miles and was accessible from the boarding facility.

On a hot afternoon in July, I was riding a 5-year-old red gelding on the canal road. He had been ridden before by his former owner, and he knew just enough to know who was boss. *He* was! Not to mention, he was as lazy as they come.

I had had a horse like him at the dude ranch that we had called *Ironsides*. I was doing everything I could to get him into a trot—spanking his rump with my leather "accelerators" about every other step plus a few rounds of explicit name calling. It took some doing, but eventually, he began to move out.

About an eighth of a mile down the road, I was beginning to sing my praise as he started to speed up. The fact that I can't sing a lick should have given me fair warning, but no, not that day. And then "it" happened—the whole world was still, my legs flew open, my neck cranked back, and my elbows stuck out like wings. I was hovering over the New York Canal on a four-legged helicopter that I knew would come crashing down. Bang! Boom! What a splash! Down, down, down we went into the icy, cold water. As we broke surface, I thought of Aristotle, Galileo, and Newton's theories of gravity—*What goes up, must come down,* and it made me a nervous wreck! Well, actually, I didn't have time to think, but I sure was sweating out going down into that murky water again. But my ride was as calm as the top of the water had been before we torpedoed its surface, and he began to win my confidence, and I began to relax.

Furthermore, while he may not have wanted to trot, he sure seemed to be enjoying the swim!

We were headed downstream, which was a good thing for I knew that the concrete embankment lining the waters of the New York Canal would eventually turn into sandy dirt. I also knew there was something wrong with this picture. The embankment was almost straight up, and I wasn't at all sure if Red could climb. He would have to pull himself and *me* up a ten-foot wall. I didn't want to end up like Humpty-Dumpty. After exhausting every bit of schooling I'd ever had in geometry, science, and accounting (the percentage of surviving this fiasco multiplied by the x-y axis equals the ratio of a snowball's chance in . . .), I scanned my brain for the infamous *Plan B*.

There was a bridge a ways down. If I could time it just right and stand up in the saddle, I might be able to grab something and pull myself up. If I missed, I would lose my ride and as the current was strong, I knew that without him, I wouldn't last long. Back to *Plan A*. When I reached the dirt embankment, I would start him up, hold on, and hope for the best. It may not have been the most methodical plan, but I had a lot of motivation on my side. As Roosevelt said, "We have nothing to fear, but fear itself," and right then, I was mighty afraid!

We reached the end of the concrete. I took one last look around hoping someone had seen us go in and would come to our rescue, but there was no one in sight. Taking a deep breath, I grabbed his mane with one hand and the saddle-horn with the other, kicking my feet away from the stirrups just in case he couldn't make it. I said a quick and earnest prayer, and up we went. He took one big lunge and his front legs were out of the water then another, and we were on the bank looking straight up. He stopped. Time stopped. Taking a large, long breath, he heaved himself into the loose dirt. Three more jumps and we were up. We stood there for quite some time. I kept thinking how blessed I was to come out of that alive, and then I remembered—Red belonged to a preacher. I sure felt baptized that day!

I learned later that Red had come from a very nice home. He had a large, green pasture in which to frolic and play with a long, rolling stream running through it. On hot summer days, Red would plunge himself into the stream to cool off. I rode Red for a couple more months, but never again on the ditch bank.

7

Practice Makes Perfect— Almost!

I'm not sure I believe in being perfect, but I sure do believe in practice. "If at first you don't succeed, try, and try again," is an inspirational quote that is the underpinning to never giving up. In my professional horse-training career, *try again* became the foundation by which everything else was built.

Now into my second year as a "practicing" professional horse trainer, I must have been doing something right. There were plenty of horses to ride, and I was gaining confidence each day. But deep down inside, I knew I had plenty more to learn. Every time I thought I had it all figured out, something would happen or a new horse would come in and prove me wrong. At that time, I could never have known that it would always be this way.

It was an experimental time for me. I read every training book I could get my hands on and tried every technique known to man, and I'm sure even a few that weren't. When I wasn't riding a horse, I was thinking about it, and by the end of the day, I was exhausted.

The good part was that getting off one horse and onto another was forcing me to become a better rider. Every horse has a different feel and a distinctive way of moving. The rider must be able to continually adjust, and I was constantly reminding myself of that. Riding a colt that had only three or four rides and then climbing onto one that had forty or fifty was and is quite a transformation and takes years to master. In the beginning, I couldn't worry or think about years. I was just trying to master the day! But even as difficult as it was both mentally and physically, I was more than up for the task and couldn't wait for the next day to discover what I might learn.

During this time, I began to experiment with equipment as well. When I first started training, I owned three bits—a smooth snaffle, a Tom Thumb snaffle, and a grazing bit. I also experimented with leverage devices such as draw-reins, martingales, and tie-downs. I grew up in an age where the term "tough-mouth horses" was used a lot. Now I believe that there is no such thing as a tough-mouth horse, only tough-handed riders. It is easy to get caught up into a pulling contest with a horse, but I can guarantee, you will not win. I have seen horses that have become so hard-mouthed that a 200-pound man pulling with all his might couldn't stop them. Let's face it, if you could stop a horse by pulling on them, they would all be stopping. There's always more to anything than what meets the eye.

Horse training equipment has evolved dramatically over time. In the past, there weren't all the choices that there are today, and certainly not the quality. There are so many different kinds of bits and spurs that it can get very confusing to know which one to use. It's kind of like choosing a doctor; with all the specialists out there, you almost have to be a doctor to know what doctor to go to!

Over the years, I have acquired many pieces of equipment for training horses and, at one time or another, have used them all. There have been times when just a simple bit change, the use of a leverage device, or a different kind of spur would make a big difference in the progression of a horse. Other times, I'd make a mistake and choose the wrong equipment at the wrong time, and any headway I had made would go south or stop altogether.

Overpowering a horse with the use of equipment is never the answer, but the right equipment at the right time can bring amazing results. Training a horse is mechanical *and* methodical, and both should be used wisely.

We have all heard the old saying, "Never look a gift horse in the mouth." The truth of the matter is we should look every horse in the mouth! A real horseman can tell you there's a lot to be learned by studying a horse's mouth and tongue. Horses' mouths can differ simply by the breed they are. Some mouths are long, some small, some wide. A standard horse bit is five inches wide, but that doesn't mean every horse can take a five-inch bit and be comfortable.

Tongues are different sizes and shapes also. Some are thick, some thin and more sensitive. Some bits work off of various degrees of tongue pressure. Knowing your horse's sensitivity can go a long way in the choosing of a bit and the adjustment of the curb strap.

As a young 19 year old, I had never touched a horse's tongue before. An old horse on our dude string began to choke. I reached in to clean his mouth out of debris when I felt a "hand-like" tongue grab *my* hand with its small fingers and thumb. It scared me to death! That was the first of too many scarred tongues that I would see over the years. Please, please be careful and seek help when needed.

8

Crossroads

Sometimes in life, you will cross paths with someone who will either say or do something that will stay with you your entire life. What you learn from them can be underappreciated at the time, even unexpected.

I know that when my wife dragged me to a luncheon over twenty years ago, the last thing I expected was to learn anything, especially from a feisty old woman in her late sixties. Seated across from us, she began some small talk asking me what I did for a living. When I replied that I trained horses, she looked shocked.

Staring me straight in the eye, she said without any hint of apology, "For some reason, I thought you looked smarter than that."

We would soon find out that she and her husband had a long history with race horses and that she thought, among other things, training horses was a dangerous occupation. By that time in my training career, I had started a few colts for the track, and I assured her that it was not the direction I was headed. But still, I could see the worry and apprehension on her face. It was a look I would remember a few weeks later.

I was outside riding on a beautiful Sunday afternoon, Mother's Day, 1989. The crisp blue sky radiated the warmth of the sun upon my back. It was a day to be celebrated—my mother for giving me life, my children's mother for giving me love.

Spring had come to Southwestern Idaho and with it, new growth and new life. That should have been enough to take a day and relax, but a new horse had come in that was giving me problems. I usually didn't ride on Sundays, but since my family was all content to enjoy the day, I thought I'd take him for a little ride to help him relax. He had been nervous, wanting to take hold of the bit and jig around. There was a 40-acre pasture right across the road, and I thought a walk out in the open might help him. An hour later, I wasn't having any luck; he was still very nervous and now dripping with sweat.

When I reached the barn, my wife came outside, and we began to talk. The horse stood there patiently, seeming to relax and calm down. I think I was relaxed too for that one pivotal moment in a sort of freeze-time before everything in life changes, as they say, in an instant. Neither my wife nor I saw it coming.

For no apparent reason, the horse made a sudden move, and I picked up my reins to check him back. What happened next came so fast; I can honestly say I didn't have a chance. Like a breaching whale, he jumped off the ground, all four legs in the air, turned over on his back, smashing down onto the hard-packed dirt and gravel. He got up, but I didn't. For the first few seconds, I knew I was in serious trouble because I couldn't move from the waist down. Then the pain hit, and I knew nothing else.

I laid there wailing and screaming, crying out to my wife, who at first couldn't process what had happened and that I was hurt. Fragile seconds ticked away until she finally gained enough composure to get help. Terrified, she tore across the road to the nearest phone, called 911, and then sprinted to our friends who were outside doing chores. By then, she was crying, hardly able to get the frozen words from her mouth,

"Steve's hurt! Bad! Help me!" They dropped everything, jumping into their pickup, ripping across gravel roads to my aid. The horse had bolted a 1/2 mile down the street before a young woman caught him and, seeing the empty saddle, knew something was wrong. Calming him enough to pen him up, she immediately threw blankets into her car and came to assist. Our poor children were so confused; one minute they had been happily playing outside, now Dad was on the ground moaning, Mom was crying, and they were being whisked away into the arms of our friends.

The ambulance had been dispatched from Boise, which was a 25-minute drive, and the whole time, I lay on the ground in intense, surging pain. One leg was bent at the knee, the other flat. I tried lying the leg down to get more comfortable, but just the slightest movement would intensify my misery. When the EMTs came, they also tried straightening it in order to help lift me onto a backboard and get me in the ambulance. One touch and I was screaming. I rode the whole way to the hospital with my knee bent, IVs in, pain-reducing drugs pulsating relief into my weary and damaged body.

I came close to losing my life that day. Somehow, I had managed to shift a fraction of an inch as the horse was coming down on top of me. According to my doctor, it was that miniscule move that kept the saddle horn from puncturing my chest, which would have killed me instantly. Instead, the horn had grazed my upper leg and hit the ground, absorbing some of the impact. My pelvis had absorbed the rest. It was not broken, but it was fractured, which meant it was severely separated.

When the doctor showed my wife the x-rays, he explained, "Your husband's pelvis has been separated about as wide as you go before it breaks, and *all* of his ligaments and muscles have been torn by impact. He's actually quite lucky, but it will take him months to recuperate."

Recuperation after surgery is one thing. It's a choice you make, inevitable and planned for, both emotionally and physically. But recuperation after a traumatic accident is another story. I was in the ICU ward for ten days. My wife and children went back to work and school, visiting me every night. But during the day, when I wasn't in a drug-induced sleep, I had a lot of hours to lie there and think. I couldn't get the image of that horse jumping up and turning over on top of me out of my head. The more I envisioned it, the more I could not imagine ever getting on a horse again.

I had been hurt by horses before—broken arm, broken leg and toes. I had even been kicked in the head once and had spent several days in a hospital recovering from a concussion. But this time was different. Whether it was my age or thinking about my family or the pain, this time, I was just plain scared. Now what? I had a million questions and no answers.

Coming home from a battle that was only beginning, I felt overwhelmed, not only with the pain, but what I would do next in life. All I had ever done and known to do was work with horses. Yet now, the road ahead was vacant, uncertain at best. The only way to deal with my trauma, both physical and invisible, was to sleep and take pain pills. A physical therapist friend of mine told me that sleep was the body's way of healing. Without knowing it, I laid in bed sleeping and healing with a specially-designed belt wrapped around my pelvis to pull me back together. My wife put a TV tray next to my bed, and my little girl placed a tiny bell by me that had a picture of a bronc-rider on it.

"Ring that, Daddy. Anytime you need help, I'll be there." And she was.

We sent the training horses back to their owners, and my wife and son fed and watered those remaining at the boarding facility. Gradually, I sat up, and eventually, on crutches, got up, doing what I could to help around the place, which wasn't that much. Three weeks later, I took ten steps across the kitchen on my own. The road of recovery was slow and painful. I didn't know where it would take me, only that I needed to walk it.

As I was healing, the time was quickly approaching when I would have to go back to work. And keeping pace with the healing was the terror. My stomach would tie in knots, and a deep-seated panic welled up inside just thinking about riding. At that time, I chewed tobacco, and although I don't recommend it, I believe it's what saved me—one can at a time and way too many. It seemed to calm my nerves, so I chewed away.

When the doctor finally cleared me to ride again, I spent several days on an old broke horse in a round pen, but even this made me nervous. My confidence shaken, my age of innocence was over. I only felt safe on certain horses. What once was nothing but joy and passion had been tainted, infected with the unseen poison of gripping, choking, paralyzing fear. The only way to face it was one hesitant ride at a time.

Months later, I learned that the horse I had been riding the day I got hurt had been raced on the track extensively the previous summer. Maybe if I had known that before I climbed on him, my life would have been different. Maybe I wouldn't have ridden him, but then, maybe I wouldn't have reached the crossroads. Yawning before me were two distinct directions my life could take— *Get in* or *Get out.* I stayed in.

I have two permanent reminders of that day. On my upper right thigh, there is a fixed dent where the saddle horn first hit. Seeing it reminds me of the pain I endured. And sitting on a shelf behind my recliner is that bell my little daughter gave me. Whenever I hear it ring, I think about life-changing instances, the miracle of healing, and choosing the right direction.

9

Saint Charlie

When you choose a new direction in life, you may have the advantage of hindsight—where you don't want to go, but you don't have foresight—you can't see every bump in the road.

After my accident, things weren't the same. I kept riding horses for a lot of reasons, but the most important one was to feed my family. I was fighting a war and, like a good soldier, I marched on.

I quit taking older horses that might have problems. I knew then that I didn't have the skills to deal with them. I had developed a new-found respect for the beast I was trying to tame. I trusted the colts more; most didn't come with a lot of trauma and baggage.

In those days, most people didn't start a colt until they were three or four years of age. By then, they were big and strong with opinions. They were different than today's horses. If you made a mistake, they would let you know it. You had to pay attention to what they were saying. Although there were no guarantees by taking only young horses, at least what they knew and learned about being ridden would be totally in my hands.

There's nothing natural to a horse when it comes to being ridden. It's really just the opposite. A horse's natural instinct is to resist, so whether it is a good or bad experience rests upon who's doing the training. If I was going to be hurt again, now it would be on my terms.

Before I got hurt, another trainer had come into the boarding facility. He specialized in training Arabian show horses for English pleasure and driving classes. Although he was very pleasant, he stayed mainly to himself, and I never paid much attention to what he was doing.

In those days, when I started a colt, it was all about getting on. A few days of ground work and up I'd go. This new guy had another method. He would drive his horses in a round pen for weeks at a time. Quite frankly, I couldn't see the point, but given my recent experience, I was now interested. I swallowed my pride and went over to the round pen where he was driving a horse. It was different this time— *I* was different. This time, I had my eyes wide open.

He was in his late fifties and in good shape for his age. Nothing about him looked like a cowboy; as a matter of fact, he could have easily passed as a banker. He didn't seem surprised to see me. I don't know if it was because I had been hurt, but when I began to ask questions about his training methods, he was an open book. He was very confident; it was obvious that he believed in what he was doing.

He was driving a colt on long lines made of a flat nylon about 25-feet long, one on each side of the horse. They went through the rings of a surcingle—a strap of sorts that goes around a horse's back, fastening under its belly. It has a number of rings on each side to allow for various adjustments where you can run your lines. On top of the surcingle is also a ring. In this case, the trainer had a cord that was attached to this ring that ran up into the bridle where it split off and ran down each side, connecting to a snaffle bit. This is called an over-check and it's used to keep a horse's head up, which was very common when driving a horse in harness.

When he began putting the colt through its paces, I have to admit, it was impressive. He could make that colt dance! He began explaining to me what he thought were the advantages to this method. According to him, there were many, one being it was safer. His name was Charlie, but at the time, I could have sworn he said, "Saint Peter"!

The next day, I purchased the best surcingle I could afford, which just happened to be the cheapest one they made. Charlie's surcingle had been made of sturdy leather;

mine was made of flimsy nylon. My driving lines were two 25-foot, 3/8" ropes with two snaps taped to each end. It wasn't pretty, but it would do for now. Running the lines through my brand new surcingle, I stood back with one in each hand ready for the miracle to begin. It only took a few minutes to realize it wasn't going to happen that day. Not only was my outfit ugly, but my technique was hideous. If the horse wasn't tangled up in the lines, I was. It was obvious that this was a learned skill and would take plenty of practice.

Charlie had made driving look easy. Not only did he have a line in each hand, but he also held a whip that he would crack occasionally to get the horse's attention or keep it moving forward. Without a third hand, I just couldn't imagine how I could possibly master this skill. And yet, for some reason, it felt right. I could feel the lines becoming a part of me, and I liked the way a horse could move unencumbered.

It took a lot of practice on a lot of horses before I would begin seeing the benefits to this method. I was teaching these colts to follow their nose, to move in both directions, pushing them up into the bridle, turning them on their hocks, guiding them to move forward and back up— unfettered, free, and loose. Everything I had wanted to teach them before while in the saddle was first being experienced on the ground. That meant that when the time came to climb aboard, the horse was conditioned—ready and willing to listen and learn.

Without even knowing it, I was starting to develop a fundamental approach to training of my own. Learning to drive a horse correctly became the foundational skill I would learn and build on for the next 30 years.

Part 3
Turn Me Loose!
Chapters 10-12

10

The Crystal Ball

ortune telling has never been my expertise. If it was, I would have been Roy Rogers riding the beautiful *Trigger*. But as I've said before, I can't sing a lick that isn't off key and hard on my wife or anyone else in my general direction.

Having a crystal ball to tell my future as a horseman could have really come in handy more than several times. *I wouldn't have ridden on the ditch bank, I wouldn't have gotten on that horse who hurt me, and I surely wouldn't have taken the all-you-can-eat shrimp advertisement literally that night I couldn't walk out of Sizzlers!* I kind of wish I had met a fortune teller at the circus I went to once with my family when I was a little guy. She could have predicted all my upcoming aches and pains and peered into the glass to see my own personal road map and where my life would lead me. But as it was, I just had an older sister who *thought* she was a fortune teller and, even in a perfectly tailored silk gown and colorful scarf, did a poor imitation of prediction. For me, it was horses that provided a continual pulsing in my heart and mind, and it was horses that would direct the path I chose.

As a young trainer, I was still trying to figure out where in this big world of horses I belonged when *Presto!* Another event would enter my life that would mold and shape me. It was in the form of a snaffle bit futurity.

In the late 1980s, some of the best three-year-old horses in the country, along with the best trainers, would come to Boise, Idaho, for a three-day show. These young horses would be asked to perform three different events while being ridden two-handed and in a snaffle bit.

Being raised in the East, such events were not common. I had no idea what I was about to witness. The events then, as they are today, consisted of fence-work, which is boxing a cow at the end of the arena for a certain amount of time, turning it loose to run down the side of the fence-line while the horse and rider are in hot pursuit to outrun the cow, slip in front of it and turn it the other way. Continue that process two to three more times and then for the finale, direct the cow out into the middle of the arena and circle it both ways—first one way and then the other. Being that it is a timed event of three minutes, the rider must be aware of the time lapsing while remembering each maneuver. If the rider spent too much time boxing the cow or running it down the fence, there was no time left for circling the cow. Or, just the opposite was true if the rider's timing was off and he was left with too much time, out there circling a cow seemingly forever as the strength in the horse weakened every second. There would be a collective sigh from both horse and rider once the buzzer went off.

Another event is the herd work where horse and rider are asked to cut one cow out of a herd and keep it from running back to it for a certain amount of time. The idea was to pick a cow that would help show off the horse's ability as a cutting horse. This also being a timed event, it is important that the rider chooses the right cows and doesn't stay with a "bad cow" (meaning a cow with too little or too much motor) any longer than he needed to.

Both events were very exciting as well as unpredictable to watch as a spectator. However, as I would learn later, it became my experience that the only way anyone could really control a cow was on the grill, and even *then* it was risky!

The third and final event is the dry work, so called because it is the only event of the three where cows are not used. This is where the young horses show off their skills as reining horses, therefore the phrase *reined cow horse*. It's just you, your training, and the horse. In this competition, the horse and rider are asked to perform one of many designed reining patterns consisting of slow and fast circles that show speed control, flying lead changes, spins, rollbacks, and sliding stops. The contestants are judged according to accuracy, speed, and the willingness of the horse when performing each move. To get a horse's final score in reining, points are added or subtracted based on their performance of each maneuver.

I had never seen such a display of horsemanship in one show. Seeing is believing as they say. I was a fan immediately and couldn't wait to go back to my barn and practice some of the things I had seen. The snaffle bit futurity was all I could talk about for days afterward! Anyone who came into my barn could see that I was trying out some of the maneuvers I had seen highly-skilled horses perform on whatever I had in training. Forget that my horses didn't even know what a circle was, let alone a slow or fast one, or that my horses had perhaps never learned to stop let alone slide-stop, or even that my horses' definition of a spin was to turn 90 degrees, stop, turn 90 degrees, stop, until we slowly made our way around 360 degrees. Roll back? I knew what it was, but my horses didn't! As far as showing how my horses could back up, I felt like I was backing up like crazy in the saddle, but no movement below deck if you know what I mean.

Still, I'm pretty convincing when I want to be, and I had everyone at my barn assured that I knew what I was doing. So much so that the next day when one of my boarders told me about her friend looking for a prospect and a trainer for the next year's futurity, she asked if I would be interested?

"Why of course!" I shouted. Suddenly, I'm a *reined cow horse* trainer who had never worked a cow or run a reining pattern other than in my mind.

First things first. If I was ever going to be a reined cow horse trainer, I would need a horse, preferably a cow horse. It takes the right conformation to stand up to such demanding training at such a young age.

As fate would have it, we got a tip on a prospect which turned into another and then another. One thing we were doing right, maybe the only thing, was that we had enlisted the help of a veterinarian who knew the kind of conformation in a horse that could withstand the training. Although expensive, his knowledge proved invaluable. After several rejections of *"No, keep looking,"* he finally approved our newest selection.

The horse was an unremarkable plain brown color. Looking back, finding plain brown horses that distinguished themselves later in my career seemed to be my MO. All I can say is somebody had to love them! This one was a mixture of cow horse and thoroughbred. A local trainer, now turned breeder, had watched many futurities and, working on his herd, thought that mixing a cow horse with a thoroughbred would give the horse an edge when running a cow down the fence, which he obviously thought was missing. Hooray for him and all the great first breeders of our time! Without them, we would not be riding the wonderful horses of today. For this horse, it worked! He was talented—not only "cowy" with speed, but smart and somewhat forgiving, which was a blessing for an amateur trainer as myself. We called him *Peppy,* which came from his daddy's side, *Peppy San Badger*—a horse that was painstakingly bred by the King Ranch to achieve superiority in the cutting arena.

Breeding can be extremely helpful when selecting the right colt. A good pedigree can read like a road map especially today with the help of our Internet brain. We can easily seek out the horses that have achieved excellence in their field of expertise. For instance, if you are looking to invest several thousand dollars in the development of a rope horse, you might want to see how the great ones are bred. In the case of a futurity prospect who may be too young to ride, breeding is another tool that may help you with your selection.

One evening, a young roper began telling me all the positive attributes of his horse and, according to him, they were many. "I can back him into the box, and he will wait forever for my nod!"

When I asked him how his horse was bred, he shrugged, "I-I don't know. I don't have a clue."

I responded with, "Don't you think you might want to know? If nothing else, down the road you may have to replace him or add to your string."

"Well, y-y-es! I would!" he answered, staring at me like I was the smartest man in the room, and for that split second, maybe I was.

As the years went on and I began to develop my skills as a horseman, I would add another element to my repertoire in the choosing of a prospect. Using a 60-foot round pen or, if need be, any space that would allow me to observe a colt moving and turning freely, I would encourage them in each gait trying to detect anything they could tell me. With each flick of an ear, a twitch of the tail, the lick of their lips, I could tell something of their temperament.

Watching a horse play in a round pen or pasture can tell a trained eye how athletic a horse is, what kind of mover they are, if the colt is fluid, how it stops, turns, or changes, or leads naturally. It can even answer if it has that presence about them that might catch a judge's eye. Since there is not a perfect horse, you have to consider what you can live with or without. Of course, no one wants to put time, money, and energy into the bloodlines of *"I don't want to"* by *"You can't make me."*

11

The Lope Around

Outside the sleepy little town of Glenns Ferry, Idaho, lies their fairgrounds. It seems every locality has a fairground arena in various states of repair standing as an ancient ghost to days gone by. And for me, this fairground will forever remain etched in my memory as the place where history was made—*my* history.

It was there I made my debut in my first competition as a reined cow-horse trainer, and my introduction into what I would forever name, *The Lope Around*. For those of you who have shown and competed in a horse event, it needs no introduction, and for those who have never had the experience, it can only be explained as a giant-sized carousel spinning around and around. As more and more riders enter the arena to warm up their horses before competing, colorful clothes, hats, and ponies bob up and down in syncopated rhythm.

I think that *the lope around* is very musical in nature, although the riders generally say little or nothing at all. But just because there are no physical sounds doesn't mean there isn't ear-splitting tension as riders focus on the task at hand—loosening their horse's muscles, seeking that right balance between too much and not enough. The act itself is a science, and equine competitions have been won or lost by this seemingly simple, but complex, act. Too much and you have a tired horse. Too little and your horse is on edge ready to blow past all its carefully rehearsed moves. I'm sure you've heard it in any classical venue—too much forte, and the beauty of the musical piece is ruined. Too little, and the music is lost.

Long before a young, inexperienced colt becomes a masterpiece, it takes a seasoned trainer to know which buttons to push. At the time I was competing in Glenns Ferry, a seasoned trainer I was not. It is difficult to take a horse somewhere you yourself have never been. I was wound pretty tight, focused on pushing this button and that, trying to find the right balance. I was the first rider to enter the warm-up arena wanting to give myself as much time as I could to figure out my horse. After a few lopes around, we both began to relax, and I started to look here and there at the other competitors. Some were pulling on their cinches, others hopping aboard their mounts, and some were beginning to enter the arena by ones and twos until very subtly, the hoofbeats of 25 horses began to lope around in time, all going in the same direction, competitors in front and back of me, creating a soothing rhythm. Although my nerves had not completely settled, my mind was content; the sun was shining in a cloudless blue sky, and I felt lucky to be a horseback on a beautiful April morning. I was relaxed enough to see the beauty of the moment, to savor the harmonious symphonic melody of the equine orchestra parading around the carousel. But just like a real carousel coming to a slow, grinding halt due to mechanical failure, our ride was about to come unhinged and our harmonious melody a musical catastrophe of riders in disarray!

To this day I can't tell you who he was—just a local cowboy was the talk. I never saw his face, and he didn't say a word, but that we all heard him was undeniable. He was the last rider to enter the arena, an aura of confident competence about him. There, in the middle of his cinch, he had tied the pièce de résistance—a tiny golden bell.

Suddenly, it was like Moses parting the Red Sea; horses and riders flew to the end of the arena and everywhere life interrupted! We were all grabbing for leather or anything that could keep us in the saddle. I have to say that for a few seconds we were a tight-knit bunch—all huddled up in a corner, trying to spur our way out. And all the while was the cowboy who rode in, seemingly unaware of the havoc he had caused, loping his horse between and around everyone without a care in the world. It took a while but eventually, our colts got used to the jingle, and the giant carousel rhythm began again. No one said anything to the rider with the bell. It was a training moment furnished free of charge from the locals, the first of many I would receive, compliments of the lope around.

Carousel. Musical. Rhythmic. In the years I have shown horses, I would say that those words sum up the feelings a rider gets on horseback when they are a part of the lope around. Unless there's someone trying to clear the arena with his golden bell, it's a pattern that doesn't change. Tranquil. Quiet. Calm. It's similar to the calm in the eye of the storm. But you don't have to be filming a new segment for *Storm Chasers* to know that the eye is only the beginning. It doesn't mean the storm is over. Things can and often do get worse. They become the most intense part of a tumultuous situation. And the giant carousel can become a massive roller coaster full of ups and downs, eye-opening even.

I had one of those moments when I was warming up for a reining class at a prestigious horse show. I hadn't been to a lot of shows with the word *professional* attached to it. Most competitors I rode with were after ribbons of color or candy bars and maybe a certificate they could hang on their walls or put in a scrapbook. But on this day, I felt I had arrived. These men and women weren't out for small change; they were competing for Benjamin Franklins, trophies, name recognition, photo opportunities and *gold* in the form of a barn full of clients!

I had a good horse under me and the best part was that he was mine. I had found him when he was coarse at best and, sorry to say, a bit ugly at worst. He was short, a dingy brown bay with a dirty, uncombed black mane and a head that looked like a stump to hang a halter on. Yet, "something" told me to take a chance on him. He was registered AQHA, and I paid for him with a ton of sweat equity trading out training on his owner's other horses. It took a lot of time in the saddle before he officially became ours. He was my pride and joy, the pinnacle of my life as a trainer who worked for hire but never on his own. He was an amazing and gifted athlete. Riding him was like riding a *Harley* with a motor that was always humming and purring. Of all the horses I had owned previously or since, he has been the best. I just knew he would make a difference in my career. And this particular show would prove his talents.

I was the first to enter the arena and began working out the kinks—his and mine. Intensely preoccupied practicing all the skills my horse would be judged by, I became unaware of a slow build in other riders around me. A call for my upcoming class was made over the loud speaker, signaling those of us inside the arena to make their way to a waiting area from which we would be called. Having those preliminary calls greatly assists all competitors because you have time to check your equipment, get a bite to eat or a drink of water or, as in my case, *use the bathroom!*

No problem, I thought as I collected my horse and looked up. That's when I saw that the indoor arena had filled to almost overflowing with riders. I was shocked to see a multitude of horses encircling me in a great wave of thundering hooves, flying manes, and surging riders galloping past. So big was the crowd of competitors that I was stuck in the middle with no way out! Lucky for me I had my *Harley.* When a gap would open, I'd push the accelerator and in we would go, taking another lope around.

I continued an inch at a time, working my way through the congestion, keeping my eyes on where the opened gate beaconed to aid in my relief. Around and around I went—a car on an imaginary roller coaster track. Kidneys protesting at my slow progress, I finally made it to the outside ring of horses. Horror of horrors, the gate was shut! No way out! Horses in front of me, horses in back; around we swarmed like rapids in a raging river. It was worse than a game of monopoly; every time I passed go, it was just a reminder of why I needed to get out! Then off I'd go navigating the chess board of horses. Finally, on one pass around, I saw a familiar face in the crowd of spectators. I yelled, "Help! Open the gate!" I didn't say *I have to go*, but somehow he knew it by the wincing of my face. Opening the gate as I came around from my latest pass, I shot past him even faster than I knew a Ferrari could roll, my horse sliding 20 feet into home plate. Talk about speed control, running fast circles, and sliding stops! If we had been getting judged for those maneuvers, we could have *both* checked off Grand Champion! Phew! How do you spell r-e-l-i-e-f?

Training horses has all kinds of fringe benefits. Most of them pay in the form of memories. Showing horses was never the direction my training would take. However, I would encourage anyone who wants to be a top horseman to challenge themselves to the competition of the show ring. There is no better way to achieve knowledge for both horse and rider than when asked to perform maneuvers at a competitive level while top judges critique you. Not to mention, you can learn a lot by watching and communicating with other trainers—what kind of equipment they are using, the breed of horses they are riding, new competitive venues— the information is unlimited.

There are good horsemen everywhere and then there are the great ones. They are not usually hard to find. They are the ones who seem to melt into the hide of a horse. They are old and walk with a limp. Well, not always; some don't limp! A truly great horseman has ridden the numbers; they have lived in the saddle atop thousands of horses. The best advice I could give someone just starting out into the horse-training field is to be an educated learner. Read, observe, listen, and then do and do it again. Be willing to ride all kinds of horses, not just the talented ones because often the overlooked have something to teach you. A good teacher will learn from all kinds of students. Know your limits because we all have them. I am learning every day that I ride a horse, that time in the saddle is as good as a college education. Horses are talented teachers, so be willing to listen, observe, and ride, ride, ride one more time.

12

Barns and Bars

A long time ago when I was a fledgling cowboy and novice horseshoer at Beavers Guest Ranch, I wore the weary off by visiting the establishments that provided solutions to my thirst. There was a bar a few miles west of town where new horizons of learning could be achieved and virtual reality attained just by settling up to the counter and ordering a sudsy cold one.

Many a cowboy went home from that establishment wondering if what he saw there was a figment of his imagination or just a tell-tale sign of the massive headache he had the next morning. You see, this bar had novelty, marketing, and customer appreciation all rolled into one. There in front of the hundreds of colored bottles of various spirits was a long counter measuring about 20 feet by roughly 3 feet wide. The counter was made of beautiful pine timber encased in a clear nonporous seal coating that was as shiny as the windows of a giant aquarium. And underneath it sloshed clear, cool water and in that water, goldfish swam. I kid you not. Goldfish *swam* in the counter of that bar! You don't have to believe me, but I do know for certain that there are at least a dozen other cowboys that can verify it as gospel.

I had to tell you the story of the goldfish bar because when you are a horse trainer, the barns you find yourself in can be just as remarkable. Becoming a trainer doesn't automatically guarantee that you'll have the finest of training facilities in which to ride. It's horses that are the teachers, and they instruct wherever class is in session. A lot of the time, a young trainer has to rent a barn or facility and board or bring their horses to it. If that doesn't cost you money, it will cost you time through agreements you have with barn owners. If that gets you down and you wonder if you'll ever be successful, just remember, Jesus was born in a stable. A lot of the barns I got myself into eventually made me stable!

Time was moving right along for me as a trainer at the boarding facility I was managing. With the march of time, there usually comes change. The facility was starting to grow, and I was riding and training a lot of horses. But as I neared my fourth year being there, it was getting harder and harder to do both. As a family, we had settled into our new world in southern Idaho. Our kids were doing great at the local elementary school in town where my wife was teaching. It was a good time to seek going out on my own as a trainer. We said our goodbyes and rented a home in town. That was the easy part. Finding a place to train out of was much harder. Although we had lived in Kuna, Idaho, for four years, we didn't really know anyone outside our little circle of friends, and our connections to the barn-owning public were limited.

So my wonderful wife did what any small-town gal would do. While shopping at the local hardware store, she told the owner of our problem who, in turn, told the owner of the corner store, who told the guy at the drive-in, who told the guy who owned the rental shop. *Bingo!* If the person who invented the Internet would have lived in a small town, he would have trashed it as a bad idea. In less than a day, we had a training facility. Sort of.

Two miles and about ten minutes later, there it was—a faded little barn asleep on the prairie. Tumble weeds—some nearly as tall as I was—had stopped their travel, resting here and there, scattered all around the barn and property. We had slowed down to look at it from the road, somewhat afraid that this abandoned ghost barn was where I would make my name as a professional trainer. The driveway crackled as we pulled in, slowly inching up to its yawning doors. It was dark inside, but eventually I could make it out. There were five stalls on each side, half of them with running pens where the horses could get outside. Actually, outside was already knocking on the boards hanging off of them in various states of disrepair. One look and I knew it was from years of cribbing horses. Looking at the sizes of the bite marks, the horses had been hungry! Today's forerunner to shabby chic. If only I had known the money in those saliva-slathered boards!

In the middle of the barn was a dirt area just barely big enough to ride a horse in. That would become important when winter hit; but I couldn't help but feel this barn was more suitable for training *miniature* horses! It was tight but so was my budget, and if you want something bad enough, you'll make it work.

The facility did have some advantages. Looking around outside, I saw a large outdoor fenced-in area I could use as an arena when weather permitted. However, the weeds were so tall I could barely open the gate. No matter, a little elbow grease would do the trick, but *my* elbows were getting plenty sore at all they would have to do to make this place work.

Because it was a race-horse facility at one time, there was an old green paint-chipped hot walker I could use. I soon discovered it didn't work. Still, I could use it as a place to tie a horse when they were cooling down. Kind of the opposite of what race-horse trainers used it for, but as for exercising colts, it was doing a dang good job with my kids right then! At least they were trying to have fun, but the rusty old hot walker was protesting their attempts, bellowing and screeching loud enough to wake the dead. It did. Out from an old blue tiny trailer I had mistakenly assumed was abandoned, popped a little old man.

Wrinkling shaggy eyebrows together, he grumbled, "What's that racket out here? I'm trying to sleep! That hot walker your kids are swinging on isn't a playground!"

What the heck! I thought. *Who is this guy?* As Gomer Pyle would have said, *"Surprise! Surprise! Surprise!"*

It seems the little man was a Vietnam veteran and I assumed, by the way he limped, was on some sort of disability from his service. After some questioning, we found out that he slept during the day and worked horse auctions on the weekends by selling tack for a local dealer. No one had mentioned him to me, although there was no real need to. He stayed there rent free and watched over the place, although I would place major emphasis on the word *watch*. From what I saw, he must have had some trouble with his vision!

"Name's Dewey," he stated.

We both squared off, wondering who each other was, but after I told him our story, he softened a bit and told me some history of the place.

Apparently, back in the day, the owner had some race horses they would work with at the facility. If the horses showed promise, they would take them on to Boise and run them on the track. Dewey put a new twist on our barn arrangement.

I liked my privacy. I told my wife, "I don't know—the barn would work, but I'm not sure about Sergeant Carter!"

After some pondering, I thought I should give it a try. After all, it had more plusses than minuses, and if I could get along with the so-called "caretaker," it might work. The biggest plus was that it was so close to our new home. It's like I tell people all the time who can't decide whether or not to buy a horse I have for sale, "Try to find one like it! How long would that take?" So, I took my own advice and moved in.

After weeks of clean up, I was back at the task at hand—learning to train a horse! I felt that, for now, God seemed to be on my side. I kept getting more horses in this "getting paid to learn" arrangement, and I was working hard at it. I had also built up a little clientele from my previous facility so I was able to bring a few horses with me when I moved in. They were a mixed bag of horses, but their owners all paid—even some on time, and when you're trying to make a go of it in any business, those are the *best* kind.

I loved my sleepy little barn, especially that old paint-chipped horse walker. As I pulled into the barn yard each morning, it was the first thing I would see staring back at me, talking to me, telling me its stories. How many hopes and dreams of potential superstars had been tied to those worn-out arms? What were their names, their breeds, their temperaments? Some days in the early morning hours when the black horizon gave way to a denim sky and stratus clouds misted across east to west, I could almost see them—heads bowed, walking around and around in a slow melodic circle like the hands on a clock ticking away their days, their time, their fate. Now, here I was bringing new life and new horses to be embraced by its arms.

After I would work a horse, I would tie it to the walker to cool off and learn to stand quietly. Sometimes, I would have as many as four horses tied to its arms sticking out like tree branches and, for some reason, it made me feel productive and one step closer to learning *how* to train. Sometimes, the steps I would take toward that goal were measured in inches.

I really was enjoying the feeling of being my own boss. If you have the ability in a job to tell yourself when you can eat lunch, you have found success. As a matter of fact, there is only one bad thing about it the way I see it. Something they call bills, and that terrified me. Although my wife was a school teacher, we weren't exactly rich. I had to make money or go get a job in town, and towns scared me worse than bills. I put my head down and went to work—like those big draft horses I drove in Colorado. I couldn't help thinking about them. When things got tough, they got tougher. They pulled—alone or together, never once thinking about push. So I pulled and rode whatever came my way, telling myself how blessed I was just to be on a horse every day. A lot of times I would be out riding in my newly weed-free arena in the early morning, and I would watch car after car go by. They were headed to work somewhere, and here I was at a desk staring between two ears on a leather chair with stirrups, leaning back and enjoying the view.

Years later while I was at a reining show, I would have a young trainer tell me he would rather flip burgers than ride grocery horses, meaning riding anything and everything to make your paycheck. But he was wrong. If you're getting on a horse at the beginning of a day and getting off one at the end, God likes you.

Not only did it seem that God liked me, but Sergeant Dewey was coming along just fine too. From his past had come his present, and I began to learn what a kind and gentle soul he was. Little by little, he became more interested in what I was doing. He considered himself a horseman as well so, naturally, he was curious about my methods—especially the driving.

I was now starting to take in the older horses I had previously stayed away from. There was such a demand to take these "do-overs" as I called them. They came with various problems that their owners had been unsuccessful in getting fixed. More often than not, they came with tough mouths. Some were so hardened they would clamp down on the bit like a pair of pliers after a sore tooth! Of course, that was their way of protecting themselves, and most of them had been protecting themselves for a long time. As far as they were concerned, it was working for them so why change?

I started my training of a horse through the use of the driving lines, and with each horse, I was becoming increasingly skilled at it. Every horse made me better at them, but even on the lines and the benefit of leverage, I could barely hold some of these horses. They would pull me around by their mouths like I was skiing behind a boat. They say you can never have too much horse power, but I'm not sure I agree. At times, I would look behind me and see the ski marks where I had been dragged—the heels of my boots digging in leaving the imprint of a lost cause. The trouble with horses, as I'm sure most psychiatrists would concur when dealing with people, is that they may have the same problems, but each one deals with it differently. Not all horses with tough mouths would arch their back, open their mouths, and plow right in. Some would rise up and back off the bit, which hollowed out their back making it difficult to guide them. Now we have different horses with the same problem, but a different fix. Tricky. Tricky. Tricky.

Once, a client brought me his rope horse and, although he was still riding and roping off of him, could feel something wasn't right. He brought the horse over to my barn, and I told him if he wasn't in a hurry I would put the horse on the driving lines, and he could watch. That way, we could talk about what the horse needed. He had been riding the horse with a curb bit, but for that day, I went back to the basics and used a snaffle bit. A lot of times when you are having problems with a horse, going back to the basics and using a bit with least resistance will unearth exactly what the problems are. Using this type of bit will show exactly what the horse knows when you take away the leverage of a more complicated bit. But I caution, *not always.*

As I snapped the driving lines through the bit and ran them through the rings of the surcingle, I could feel the horse's nervous tension in my hands. By now, I had held enough lines in my hands where I was starting to feel things. Horses, like people, can have unique ways of communicating through their mouth. I like to think horses are like children when they are trying to get your attention. The only difference is 900 pounds or more, and in the horse's case, the size is a game changer.

As I gathered the lines and clucked to him, the horse went forward, but as soon as he hit the end of the reins and felt the bit, his eyes rolled back in his head and panic struck and up he went—all four feet off the ground! Incredulously, he wasn't finished! He rolled over in mid-air then hit the ground with his back, slamming his head into the dirt so hard he nearly knocked himself out! Watching his fear and power enfold made me flash back to only a few years prior; if I had been on *this* horse when my accident happened, I would not have survived. My client looked at me, and we both knew he had been sitting on a time bomb ready to detonate. The timer for this horse was ticking to go off at the precise time I had him on the lines. That was the day I was again reminded about the importance of groundwork when training a horse. That was the day my client learned it too.

I spent a lot of time at that barn riding around in circles and in the winter when I was stuck inside, *tight* circles. I would come to appreciate the value of them in the development of any horse, young or old. Young horses don't know what you want them to do. You are their first teacher. A good teacher continues to learn *how* to instruct. Older horses often missed these first opportunities, and their learning curve was usually greater. It would be amazing to me when I got on older horses—even those that had been ridden a lot—how little they knew when asked to just walk in a circle. How difficult it could be? And when asked to trot in a circle, it was almost impossible. Think about it; when a horse is turned out in the open, do they walk, trot, or even lope around in a circle? No. It's not natural for them. They will stop and roll back over their hocks and switch leads, even back up occasionally, but not circles. It is a *learned* skill, and since so many other things can be introduced from the circle—such as the turn-around, the two-track, speed control, and forward motion. They are essential to foundational training. Good circles, as any reining horse trainer will tell you, look easy. But looks can be deceiving. There is a lot going on there for both horse and rider. The key to good circles is for the rider to learn to ride the whole horse. It is easy to get caught up into just riding one part of a horse at a time. A lot of horses encourage this by their unwillingness to yield.

For me, I began breaking the horse down into three parts: front, which includes the mouth, neck, and shoulders; the middle, which includes the back, rib cage, and belly; and the hip. The most forgotten part of the horse is the hip, and yet it is very important for it is the rudder and the motor and must be engaged to complete the circle. Those three parts work together, teaching the horse to guide, pull, bend, lift, and follow.

The simplest of things I can compare it to is paddling a canoe. If you paddle it from the front, the drive of the oar and your weight raises the back end out of the water forcing downward motion with lots of resistance. If you paddle from the middle, the canoe will bow and hollow out making it hard to control. But if you paddle from the back with your weight raising the boat out of the water distributing the weight of the canoe, then every stroke of the oar creates forward motion. Something to think about and I was thinking about it all the time.

Looking back, I can't begin to tell you how much I enjoyed that little barn on the prairie. There were a lot of reasons why I did, but mostly it was the privacy. After running a public stable and scheduling around boarders and even at times dealing with opinions from the owners of the boarding facility, I cherished the independence the little barn allowed me. Even Dewey was refreshing—someone to talk to at times, yet he offered no opinion. Life, for both of us, went on—he, in his little trailer, and me on the back of a horse going around and around and around.

I spent three years there driving horses, riding, doing whatever it took to perfect my skills as a horse trainer. It was working. I was getting horses, so much so that I was filling every stall and outdoor pen on the property. That was a good thing, or so I thought. Although the owner of the barn never came around much, I would send him a check every month for rent. But that didn't mean he wasn't watching, and one day he approached me with his thoughts. Since I was doing so well, he saw no reason why he shouldn't *share* in the wealth which, unfortunately, led to a dilemma for me. Something the business world refers to as profit margin. Once again, the small-town hotline would come to my rescue. Through connections I had made, someone knew someone else who knew of a larger barn and arena where the owner was letting the public ride for a nominal fee. The good news is that trainers were welcome!

By September of that year, I was settled into my *new* barn—a stark contrast from the quiet, sleepy little barn. Although many times the size, the bigger barn came with baggage. Typical of a public arena, for a few bucks and using the honor system (which mostly went dishonored), anyone could ride there anytime. In they would come, dragging their horses behind them and occasionally being drug in by their horses! In those days of limited places to ride during winter months, the horse-owning public provided me with plenty of entertainment. I never knew what to expect next or when the action would start. The friendly buckskin would become a snort-blowing, slobbering bronco and, in two jumps, plant their rider in the ground. Watching in disbelief, I'd rush over to investigate, only to have the rider jump up to inform me, *"He's never done that before!"*

Right, I'd think to myself. I've heard that once or twice (generally on a weekly basis). There were times I'd be riding a colt and see loose horses running around dragging their lead ropes behind. They had broken loose from their owner, playing cat and mouse with whoever tried to catch them—ducking away as soon as someone reached for their halter.

With all the commotion, my easy-going colt turned spasmodic. Now *I* was looking for a spot to bail! As soon as my feet hit the ground, I was caught up in the game: chasing my own horse.

One fellow—for reasons I still don't know—always got on his saddled horse on the concrete pad in front of the arena gate. And every time he would swing his leg over, his horse took to bucking and skating across the concrete like a cow on ice! Time after time this happened. I never understood which was harder, the concrete or his head.

Not only did I have to watch out for any number of strange people, but there were other trainers just like me that came with a string of horses to work. All of us were sharing time and space in one corner or another allowing me to watch my peers in action. Back in those days, there wasn't the information overload like there is now, so trial and error seemed to be the method of choice. Techniques I had seen before, and others I had never seen or *hope* to ever see again, were part of my everyday learning curve.

The trainers who made me the most nervous were a husband and wife team who lived right next door to the arena and had been training out of it for many years. They were world-class trainers with many world-class horses to their names winning classes in Halter, Pleasure, and Reining. They both had a reputation of keeping to themselves and sometimes being downright unfriendly.

I enjoyed watching them ride their beautiful pleasure horses. They had them going low and slow without using draw reins, running martingales, or other such mechanical devices. Although I had no real interest in pleasure horses, I paid attention when I saw collection in a horse, and they certainly had their horses collected. Heads down, backs up, their horses moved as if suspended in air. I found myself listening and stealing peeks, although that didn't seem to be a problem. It was doubtful those trainers ever noticed me at all.

One day, I was in a learning tug-of-war with my latest prospect—a queening horse who thought he was king. I was trying to get him ready for a rodeo queen competition, and I was working like a mad man on lead changes, and he was informing me in no uncertain terms that he was not in the least bit interested in changing leads. The last thing a budding horse trainer wants is to let a potential queen candidate down. So the game was on—me (150 pounds soaking wet) versus a 1000-pound fiery red, smoking-chrome gelding. That creamy white mane and tail gave him plenty of attitude when it came to *not* performing a lead change. I had just about given up, completely worn out from my efforts, when the voice of, dare I say, *"God"* came out of the corner of the arena.

"He's dropping his shoulder."

I looked up, horror struck that I might be meeting my "Maker," so to speak, and there he was—not God, but the trainer next door.

I didn't even know he had a voice, much less an opinion about what I was doing. I could do nothing but listen as for the next 40 minutes he schooled me on the dos and don'ts of lead changes, and I got the riding lesson of a lifetime. The next day, my new found trainer-friend came riding by, and I asked him how I looked.

"I can only hope I look as good on a horse as you," he said and, without another word, rode off to the other side of the arena.

What a compliment! Thinking I had bridged the communication barrier between us, I was ready to learn more. But I soon figured out his compliments, let alone *words,* were few and far between. For two long months, chit-chat was minimal. We both had work to do.

One day I was driving one of my colts in the corner of the arena. A large shadow rode by on a beautiful horse and stopped, looming over me. "How much would it cost to put one of my horses on those lines for a few weeks?"

I was so taken back that I stammered, "Why, for you—not a thing!" The next day, his colt was tied to a post in front of my tack room. Without a word, the man had given me his approval as a horseman.

The colt really was stunning; even in the early morning darkness, he shone like burnished bronze. As I worked with his colt, I began to find the problems—holes that a set of lines could find. The horse was abrasive which, in the saddle, keeps them locked and resistant. I would have to break him free, and it wasn't easy. Several weeks went by. I would occasionally see the trainer loping by, stealing a glance in my direction. He never said a word and, eventually, I got the horse to yield to the lines. I walked the colt back to the man's barn behind the arena and handed him the lead rope.

"Thanks," he said, and it became clear he wasn't saying anything more.

With the passage of time, whenever I'd see the man ride that colt in the arena, I, too, would steal a glance. I wondered how I had done. Had I helped the colt? Could his trainer feel the lightness I had eventually achieved with the driving lines?

One evening, I was packing up to leave for the day. Tired, hungry, I was ready to go home. Darkness was seeping into the cracks in the roof and finding every corner in that big empty arena. Hearing the familiar buzzing as the indoor lights warmed and flickered on, I looked up to see a man on horseback coming out of the darkness straight toward me. Like an old projector pitter-patting a new movie scene, the lights revealed not a stranger but my neighbor on the colt I had driven.

"You helped him, you know. He's different. Better."

Suddenly, I wasn't tired anymore. Matter of fact, I kind of lifted off the ground as a feeling of pride swelled inside. "Good!" I yelled to my neighbor's back as he trotted away.

I knew he gave out few compliments. I wouldn't have received one if I hadn't earned it. Nor would I have wanted it. Pride gave way to happiness. I finally realized I had made the right decision after my accident. Having earned the respect of one of the greatest horseman in the world, I was realizing that I, too, had skills.

From that moment on, the man of few words and I became co-laborers in our chosen profession. There were times when things would happen with different horses, and we would help each other, offering a joint form of mentorship and differing points of view. Sometimes, I'd loan him a bit that was giving me good results. Other times, we would both watch each other ride.

One of the most essential skills he taught me was the importance of good ground in an arena. If it's too deep, your horses could get pulled tendons, too shallow and there isn't enough protection. In that barn, I learned how to make good ground out of mud.

Anytime you are working in an old and weathered facility, new problems creep in. I didn't notice it during the long Indian summer we had, but as soon as the weather changed from sunshine to rain, snow, or sleet, the clouds magically appeared inside and right above our heads. Gusts of wind tore at loose flaps of metal roofing, hammering them against the wooden frame. With each thrust, a river of water streamed onto the ground creating a pond of quicksand that made riding perilous. But to my trainer friend and his wife, it wasn't anything. They knew what to do.

There were plenty of filled stalls right next door with used shavings in them. Pine or cedar shavings in a horse's stall are often used as bedding and waste management. Not only are used shavings excellent sources of mulch, but they have a cushioning and absorbent nature. We hauled wheelbarrows full of it into the center of the arena in a worker-ant fashion—scoop, haul, and dump over and over until the pile was big enough. Then, using a tractor, we would work the shavings into the mud until they made a light, feathery powder that was like riding on a cloud. It was a process that would take most of the day with all three of us working nonstop. Resting on top of shovels or rakes, we'd admire our work until another deluge of winter and real clouds would open up, and the process would begin again. Frustrations aside, the three of us were becoming good barn-mates.

Becoming neighborly with them had some fringe benefits. One day while saddling up my next horse, the trainer's wife surprised me with an offer. She had realized how curious I was about their world-winning pleasure horses. She handed me the reins of an older, seasoned horse. Up I went and the low, slow cadence took on a gait of its own. Over the years, I had only minimal tastings of that gait but never to this point of perfection. A click of the tongue or the smallest of commands from its rider set this polished steed into motion, and I was soon drifting along on a magic carpet ride. It was breathtaking atop that steed, and it was difficult to get off. Once I did, the view from above stayed with me. I thought of the trainer who had let me ride my first light horse and how it was a feeling I would pursue and try to replicate as I learned my skilled profession. Now, here I was being given another priceless lesson from my neighbors, and all I could feel was awe and gratitude.

Elbows propped over the arena fence the next day, I watched as my trainer friends brought in their halter horses—16 hands high, 1400 pounds of solid muscles bulging and flexing like the best of body builders. I couldn't help but think of the famous body-builder, Arnold Schwarzenegger. The trainers spent countless hours teaching them to yield their front quarters upon a cue from a standing position. I'd watch as these marvelous athletes would yield to the right and left, back up, move forward, and when standing straight, have all four legs placed perfectly on the ground. Although these horses would never be ridden, their intelligence and desire to learn was evident. One could not help but feel that if Hercules had needed an equine partner, one of these horses would have fit the bill.

The beauty and style of their halter horses said a lot about these trainers. Looking back, I sometimes wonder how they did all they had to do. They were training horses to ride as well as those to show in halter classes, giving riding lessons, and if that wasn't enough, they also ran a breeding program. In the spring of the year, pens next to their barn grew up overnight; all of them filled with numerous mares to breed.

A lot of trainers would come and go out of that public arena, but I stayed. I was in a state of learning and becoming a better student. Never ever become the best horse trainer you know. If you do, you are only cheating yourself—and who knows, maybe even the neighbors next door.

Although things were never perfect in that big barn, it was beginning to feel as comfortable as my worn-out moccasins. I sat in a lot of saddles, rode and drove a lot of horses, and got used to things I would have never thought possible while in my quiet, sleepy little barn. If I were a singing cowboy, I'd compare the two like this: it was "Home on the Range" meeting "Welcome to the Jungle"!

Somewhere in the chaos, I got used to the public running in and out, the trainers coming and going, and the husband and wife team who, at times, just needed an ear to listen to their woes. Sometimes, they'd ride in, teeth gritting and mad—at a horse, at the weather, at each other, at everything, at nothing.

The man was a brittle diabetic, and there were times when his disease would get the best of him. Before I knew of his illness, I'd wonder at his erratic behavior. Later, I'd recognize the hunched shoulders, vacant stare, and angry demeanor. Sometimes, I could shake him out of it by letting him vent, but other times I just knew when to steer clear and let him work it out himself. I had no way of knowing then that his diabetes would lead to his early death at age 45. I think of him often, and I'm certain he's riding a good horse in Heaven. I like to picture him kind and relaxed without the added weariness a disease can add to a person's life. Heck, I'm real certain he's up there showing pleasure horses and giving lessons.

He'd probably say to me, "And you thought the ride was smooth on used shavings. Brother, it's not even close!" And off he'd go, cantering low and slow into the crystalline sky.

Ahh, that's a soothing and quite calming scenario. Nothing like what really happened to us while he was with us here on Earth. As it was, we were all getting used to each other in the big barn. We were becoming neighbors and friends. Life was good. Predictable, albeit the occasional catastrophe with a horse, the weather, each other, we just kept riding around in big circles. And then one day, as I pulled into the parking lot outside the arena, something was quite different. Unusual. And just like that, our riding arena changed.

Now, there were loaders and dump trucks working away inside, fashioning piles of dirt into little mountains scattered around what appeared to be a racetrack. It seemed the owner of the barn had been approached by a local bicycle club over the weekend. They needed a place for a BMX racing course, and since money talks a lot louder than horses neigh, I had no choice but to listen as the owner gave us the details: the bikes were in, and the horses were out!

Where to now? The "close your eyes and find another barn" would go on for several more years. It was a little like the game *Pin the Tail on the Donkey*, only it was more like *Pin the Trainer on the Barn*. Somehow I would always find another place, but I was getting tired of being blindfolded and spun around. The best part of this was that by the time I was in a position to build my own facility, I knew just what I wanted.

Part 4
Deep Waters
Chapters 13-14

13

"If you build it..."

Scraping accordion tentacles across the stratus-covered clouds, I watched a mammoth metal arch rise up to inhale the cold November sky. Gravity and mechanics eased it to the ground forming a colossal skeleton into the familiar shape of a horse arena. *My* arena on *my* land. The undertaking of my lifetime spent on and around horses where I had traipsed into and out of barn after barn, arena after arena, had finally culminated in the building of my own horse facility. It was amazing to watch. Unbelievable. A dream come true.

It had not been built all at once. When I first went home to train on my own land instead of renting other facilities, I had to start small. Very small. My first "barn" was a borrowed two-horse trailer for a tack room and a 60-foot round pen where I labored in all kinds of inclement weather and heat—108 degrees of heat in those hot summer months and as the songwriter, *Ian Tyson,* would say—18 inches of rain in those pre-winter months. With each passing season, I added to my own facility.

The borrowed horse trailer/tack room gave way to a concrete slab and stalls traded out in horse training with anyone who had a skill I needed. Every business does a little of that, but you have to know when and what you can live with and without.

I went several years without a roof on my barn and then later, without doors until, eventually, a six-stall barn rose up from the mud on which it started. The center portion of the barn was larger than most because I had spent many years saddling in cramped quarters. I knew from experience that I wanted room in the middle to move horses in and out easily, saddle one horse while another cooled down, as well as have a place to shoe during bad weather.

Gradually, outside pens for horses appeared, unattached to the barn and to each other. I had learned that having a space between the pens did more for preventing horses from kicking, biting, or hurting each other saving me from costly vet bills. Not to mention, no one pays you to ride a lame horse. There was a reason for everything I put into my own facility based on years of experience. Training is a skilled science. When you train horse after horse in many different facilities, you get a data-driven education. If nothing else, it's a method to your madness.

My new facility gave me a sense of success and, at the same time, a sense of freedom. Although I would always be grateful for the things I learned and the people I met in public arenas, they did take a toll on me. There was constant scheduling around other people or horse events and at any given time, my training sessions were changed or stopped because of who or what walked in the door.

"If you build it they will come," and they did! There were years of horses of every color, breed, and temperament. My wife would tell me that sometimes she would look down from our house to the outside pens and see a "run" on paints, or sorrels, palominos, bays, or buckskins. Those were the days of riding from sunup to sundown. They were the days of waiting lists for people to bring in their horses for training. Not only that, but there were multiple horse-riding lessons and clinics, preparations for horse expositions and, later, reining shows. Not only was I building a horse-training facility, but now I was building horses, a term I would come to appreciate.

If a person is going to build anything of substance, it has to have a solid foundation. My simple ABC approach became more important. As I've mentioned before, don't go to B before A, and certainly don't start at C and go to Z. If you want to build a solid horse, you must take time to make sure they understand. A horse will never follow his nose if its feet are stuck in the ground. A horse cannot round his back if it's not been taught to pick up its belly. You cannot cheat the process and, believe me, it is a process.

There are always people who are in a hurry, but if you are looking to build a quality product, sometimes the slowest way is the fastest. You will only get one chance to start a colt correctly; after that you're just fixing mistakes. You can do it fast or you can do it right, but in the training of a horse, you can't have both. A horse must be developed at its own pace. If you give a horse what it needs, it will give you what you want, and you need to have the experience to know what that is.

Every trainer who is making a living riding horses soon realizes that in order to pay the bills, they must ride a certain number. They need to develop a style using techniques that work for them. Since building a program to fit every horse is impossible, having one that can be tweaked here and there and one that the trainer has become comfortable with is the key to success.

For me, it was the driving lines. A good horse is a safe horse. The lines allowed me the ability to test and develop a lot of things at once. If a horse was stuck and wanted to rear up, I could teach forward motion, going up into the bridle instead of the air. I could teach the horse where the parts of its body were. They would learn where their feet were, how to move those feet forward, backward, how to turn on the fence, and roll over their hocks. As part of this groundwork, I would tie a plastic bag on the end of a whip to use as a conditioning tool to keep their attention.

I emphasize *conditioning* and *tool*. Conditioning is preparation for something yet to come. Its purpose is to teach or to guide a horse in a safe, contrived arena the skills it will need in *every* arena. It is no different than the conditioning athletes go through before they perform. A tool is a means to an end. It is designed to assist or to help a horse *think*. It may be an actual device, but its most important functionality is as a method or process that can lead a horse in its progression as a thinker. If you put these ideas into the realm of athletes or professional dancers, you will find that they condition all the time. Most of that conditioning uses a tool—weights, hitting blocks, or bars on which to practice maneuvers. The purpose is to be made ready to perform. Whether the performance is a football game, a ballet, a horse show, or even a safe ride on a trail horse, it is the application of skills taught that will make all the difference.

Once, I had put 90 days on a colt for a friend of mine. Thirty of those days were on the lines. My friend was getting older, and I didn't want him to get hurt. After he took the colt home and rode it for a while, he began practicing his roping on a basketball.

One day, he was invited to a branding and could not wait to catch his first calf and drag it to the fire. Building his loop as he trotted into the calf pen, he threw at one and it landed perfectly around the calf's head—just like a basketball. This time, unlike the basketball, the calf took off—hit the end of the rope, nearly pulling my friend down as he struggled to dally around the saddle horn. Feeling trapped, the calf made a bee-line for my friend's horse. He quickly realized that this was nothing like roping a basketball. The calf circled them several times getting the rope intertwined in the horse's legs, under its tail, and wrapped expertly around its rump. My friend had been captured by the calf! Both horse and rider were squatting defensibly in terror. But because during its training the colt had felt the driving lines on and around its legs and under its tail, they weathered the storm.

As the crew of other riders flew to their rescue cutting the rope from the calf, the colt stood there quietly. My friend had three offers that day to buy his colt. He refused. The colt had saved him from serious injury. Now that his rope had been cut to pieces, he never roped again—not even a basketball. Besides, both he and the colt had already become legends.

As I have mentioned before, training horses is a skilled occupation. You learn those skills on the back of a very talented teacher. As my facility grew, so did my training and my evolution as a horseman. But I was missing something, and I wasn't even sure what it was. Once again, the horse would show me the answer. Or—was it my wife?

14

Why?

As I watched his young daughter ride my lesson horse around the arena, I asked the proud father, "What do you do for a living?"

He told me he had the same factory job for the past 23 years, but to help make ends meet, he liked to do mechanic work on old cars that needed fixing up. Back in his younger days, he had raced a few cars on the local tracks.

I always liked to have one parent stay around for lessons for many reasons, and as I started hollering instructions to the young girl, it soon became clear that I wasn't the only voice in the choir. I was instructing her on how to keep the horse in its correct position, which would allow an easy transition into the next maneuver. Her father was adding his input wherever he thought he could.

This was nothing new to me. Over the years, men and women with similar backgrounds seem to catch on to the mechanical aspects of training a horse even if they had never ridden one in their lives. They have a real understanding for working parts of a machine—gears and gear progression, wheelbase, neutral, and up and down shifting. They grasp the attention needed to parts to keep a vehicle moving soundly and evenly.

The excitement builds on their new-found discovery. They begin to shout out what the rider should do for maximum performance. However, when they are challenged to get on the horse themselves and show how it is done, what looked to be the most simplest of tasks on the ground quickly turns into frustration and, more often than not, embarrassing disaster. They can see it, but it's a whole other dimension to do it. What the brain comprehends and what the body can actually perform is vastly different.

When my grandson was eight years old, he had won a spot to compete in mutton busting at our local rodeo. It wasn't easy to get selected; one had to be the right age, weight, and the right name drawn out of hundreds. He was thrilled to have been chosen and took to watching every mutton-busting video he could on the Internet. His parents prepared him to be mentally tough and emotionally ready. I had prepared him on the mechanics of staying in the middle.

The big day comes. His number is called. Up and on he goes on what looks like the biggest sheep around. The horn blasts, and out he shoots with his hand held high! Then to the side he rolled, dragged, and in a few jumps was off, face down in the dirt. He pops up, looks up at his relieved grandmother and declares, "It didn't look that fast on YouTube!"

It's never as easy as it looks. Education is more than what we learn through formulaic equations, sentence diagramming, and reading with metacognition. We learn with our brain, but we discover and give meaning to knowledge through experience.

I don't know how many nights I would come into the house after a frustrating day of training. I would get down on all fours, simulating a horse to understand what position their body should be in to perform a maneuver. As silly as it seems, there were times when this would actually give me some understanding of what they needed to do.

When my students were having a hard time grasping the concepts I was teaching, I would get behind them and pull on their ears imitating the reins and the subtle difference between leading and pulling, up and down, in and out, and what these movements could feel like to a horse. Teaching a feel is very difficult, but learning to feel transcends a rider's awareness of where a horse is going and where they need direction. It is counterintuitive to the rider to learn this advanced skill and takes time to master. Even then, there can be roadblocks to your success.

One morning, I was giving a lesson to a young lady I had known since she was in a car seat swinging on her mother's arms. I was always up front and honest with her questions. One day after practicing circles with her horse and not getting the result she wanted, she slid off her horse, kicked a rock across the arena, grimacing, "Why can't I get this? I'm doing everything right!"

"You're inconsistent!" I barked back.

"Oh, no I'm not!" she yelled. "I am *consistently* inconsistent!"

Knowing the frustration she felt, I countered, "Then let's figure out *why*."

Teaching never came easy to me at first, but one evening, my school-teacher wife came down to the arena to visit. It was never a routine for her, but I always enjoyed it when she did. Perched on top of a tractor seat and still in her professional clothing, the evening sun reflecting across her face, she took on an aura of someone in authority. Riding a colt, I began working my hands back and forth to encourage him to quit fighting the bit.

"Why are you doing that to your horse?" she asked.

"Because it works," I said, and in a short period of time, we could both see my method was working. I was now an accomplished rider. I was feeling these horses underneath me and my timing was on the mark. My horses readily responded to my cues and then relaxed. But I couldn't tell her *why*. I'm sure that was a question my wife had asked her students many times before in her own classroom. Now, she was in my classroom, and I didn't have the answer.

That night as I put my horses away, my wife's question lingered in my mind. I realized that while training horses can be seen and felt, until you can answer the question why, you will always be guessing.

From that moment on, my training took on new meaning. I learned why I worked my hands back and forth to get a horse to quit fighting the bit, to drop his head, relax in my hands, and be able to move forward. I know now that everything works off of forward motion when a horse's belly is up and its head down and collected. I know why I ride and when to ride in circles. I know why I teach a horse to back up, roll over its hocks, all the while using my legs and steady, consistent pressure on the reins. I know why I ride a horse up into the fence, or why I use a certain bit and when to use that bit. Most importantly, I know how to explain why I do the things I do and why it all works. The answers to why have shown me the truth of this fact: every day I ride a horse, I am still learning. That is *why* my definition of a professional horseman is an individual who is constantly being trained by a horse.

Why?

To sit on top of a 1000-pound horse when they begin to get light on their feet and light in your hands can stir the blood and soul of a real horseman. But it is one thing to be a gear-jammer and a totally different thing to become one of the gears.

Part 5
End of the Trail
Chapter 15

15

The End of the Trail

I'm one of those people that happen to believe that we are put on this earth for a purpose, and that we all have a destiny. I can't prove it, but I believe it. I believe John Wayne didn't just wake up and decide to be John Wayne. Or that George Strait just decided he would try and sing a little. Or that Elizabeth Taylor, one of the most beautiful women in Hollywood, went down to the local salon and said, *"Do something with my hair."* It was their destiny to be who they were. Although I do believe we have the ability to tweak our destiny a little—make small decisions, move to the left or the right, push/pull, start/stop—it is the part out of our hands and out of our control that defines who we will become.

I wanted to be a horseman long before there was an ocean of answers on how to become one streaming from the

Internet, cable TV, books, magazines, blogs, YouTube, Facebook, Tweets, Twangs, and anyone who wants to be one. You don't have to earn it through time and experience, you only have to claim it, and there seems to be a following.

In the beginning, I was waiting—to begin. I didn't know that my life with horses would span over 50 years. I only knew to get started. My passion propelled me into a future that evolved over time. I "cut my teeth" during my years as a horseshoer and manager of a dude-ranch business. Launching into my own businesses of buying/leasing dude-ranch horses, creating and running sleigh rides, and becoming a trainer formed the building blocks of who I am as a horseman.

In 1987, my family—a wife and two wonderful children—came to Idaho through some twists and turns in life we could have never predicted. Destiny came knocking, but we were too young to hear its call. We went from living the good life to living a life—a different life, full of strangers, and uncertainties.

This was the year I hung up my shingle as a horse trainer and began to try and convince the world, and myself, that I knew what in the heck I was doing. For the next several years, I would train and un-train horses every day. It was lonely and frustrating work. I'd hug my kids and kiss my wife, and off they would go to school and work. My best friend in the whole world was a dog and, I must confess, I consistently talked to her and to myself, whichever one was listening the most.

The first three years, it wasn't all that bad of an arrangement. I found my dog compassionate, and as for expert advice, well, I just asked myself. After a while, trying to figure out all the answers got old.

During my early years, I was learning a lot about how to train. At first, I stayed where everyone stays—in the shallow end or in that part of training I knew I had a handle on—the way I had always done it or the way I had always ridden a horse. But as I got more clients and touched more horses, things began to subtly shift. I was beginning to drift toward deep waters, into an area where I had no footing to hold me up. It was sink or swim, and I was dog-paddling like crazy!

It took me a lifetime of years to learn that money, fame, and the gift of good salesmanship doesn't make you a horseman. Horses make you a horseman, always have, always will. And you've got to ride the numbers before you will ever learn what their stories are and how to read them.

In the end, one naturally asks questions about their life. And once asked, the answer comes. Have I become a horse whisperer? No. But I have become a horse listener, and when they whisper, I listen.

End Note – The Last Great Fall

There are some things in life you will remember forever. Stretching across the memories of your mind you will find your parents, your first horse, your one true love, the birth of your children, and if you're lucky enough, the birth of your grandchildren. If you are an aging horseman, you will never forget the last great fall.

I was riding a nice colt on a farm road across from my facility. He liked to shy from things, but I wasn't at all worried. I had handled horses like this before—and before—and before. Whenever I am on a horse, I am fully engaged in the moment. I feel every ripple and quiver cascading down the horse's neck, shoulders, ribcage, and rump. This beautiful red sorrel gelding had belonged to my best friend until he passed from this earth. Anytime I had the opportunity to ride his horse, collective memories of our brotherly kinship and laughter streamed across the pages of my memory.

I was perfectly content, not a care in the world with the azure cloudless sky seen on thousands of horseback rides combined with the autumn splendor around me. On one side, golden corn stalks rested haphazardly against each other—remnants of summer harvest. On the other side was a field punctuated with bales of hay tempting my equine partner with its clean, fresh, green aroma appealing to even me—not for taste, but for the memories of a life spent on horses. A symphony of gratitude began stirring, and I found myself singing. *"Saddle Tramp! Saddle Tramp! I'm as free as the breeze, and I ride where I please, Saddle Tramp!"*

I had just turned 68 years old and, if I was to tell the truth, was maybe a bit top-heavy. Still, it had been many years since I had an aerial dismount. A ringtail pheasant startled in the cornstalks and flew up in front of us, beating its wings into a fluttering, whirring sound. My long-legged colt flew up into the air, almost alongside Mr. Ringtail taking me along with him. It wasn't one of those amazing rides that go up to the 8-second buzzer. It was more like right up to the 1-second buzzer. The colt ducked out from under me, and I was airborne. For a split second, I could fly! Every horseman knows what that is like, but this time, it was different. This was a mature, overweight cowboy in touch with his true feelings. Never before had I realized that this might be my last time to torpedo off a mighty steed, like so many men before. I like to think I did it with grace and a bit of class.

Just before I hit the ground, I rolled onto my back looking into the cloudless sky above me, waiting for the mighty thud. As I laid there on the ground, out of the corner of my eye, I saw the colt dragging the reins toward a lush green, bale of hay, content to stand there filling his belly. Horses have been worthy opponents as well as trusted companions. They have taught me everything I know about training them. And I believe I taught them things too.

I laid my head back down to rest on my crushed cowboy hat. Eyes tilting up toward the sky, I thought, *This time, I had nothing to prove, nothing to gain.* I had only gratitude to God for a life well lived—*between the reins.*

~For my mother~

About the Authors

Steve Huffman trained horses in the Treasure Valley of Idaho for over 30 years. Horses have been a part of his life since he was a small boy accepting his grandfather's challenge to keep a dollar bill between his seat and the saddle. Steve has shown horses, given clinics, ridden in horse-exposition shows, and developed his craft each and every day. His unique style of training is based on solid horsemanship skills between rider and horse. "There is a lot of difference between sitting on a horse and riding one," is a common statement he tells his clients. He brings his expertise and over 50 years of riding to this book about his life *between the reins.*

Carol Huffman has loved horses since her grandfather took her on an excursion through the mountains of Montana in hopes of finding that one wild horse she had requested—*"A white one with pink ears."* Although it eluded them that day, horses have become a part of her life since she first met her husband, Steve, at a Colorado dude ranch. A proud mother of two children and five wonderful grandchildren, she is a retired teacher, proprietor of many businesses, and most of all a dedicated and accomplished writer. Bringing her husband's stories to life has been pure joy as they walked down memory lane describing the ins and outs and growing pains of a horseman. This book has been written by someone who had a front row seat to a man following a passion. Through the gift of her pen, she shares their lifetime spent with horses.

You may contact both authors at their email address: **BTR Publishing** @ betweenthereins@outlook.com

They are available for training clinics, writers' conferences or club meetings/luncheons.

NOTES

NOTES

NOTES

Made in the USA
Middletown, DE
09 September 2023

37671794R00099